Praise for *Inside the Minds*

"Need-to-read inside information and analysis that will improve your bottom line—the best source in the business." – Daniel J. Moore, Member, Harris Beach LLP

"The *Inside the Minds* series is a valuable probe into the thoughts, perspectives, and techniques of accomplished professionals…" – Chuck Birenbaum, Partner, Thelen Reid & Priest

"Aspatore has tapped into a goldmine of knowledge and expertise ignored by other publishing houses." – Jack Barsky, Managing Director, Information Technology and CIO, ConEdison Solutions

"Unlike any other publisher—actual authors that are on the front lines of what is happening in industry." – Paul A. Sellers, Executive Director, National Sales, Fleet and Remarketing, Hyundai Motor America

"A snapshot of everything you need…" – Charles Koob, Co-Head of Litigation Department, Simpson Thacher & Bartlet

"Everything good books should be—honest, informative, inspiring, and incredibly well written." – Patti D. Hill, President, BlabberMouth PR

"Great information for both novices and experts." – Patrick Ennis, Partner, ARCH Venture Partners

"A rare peek behind the curtains and into the minds of the industry's best." – Brandon Baum, Partner, Cooley Godward

"Intensely personal, practical advice from seasoned deal-makers." – Mary Ann Jorgenson, Coordinator of Business Practice Area, Squire, Sanders & Dempsey

"Great practical advice and thoughtful insights." – Mark Gruhin, Partner, Schmeltzer, Aptaker & Shepard PC

"Reading about real-world strategies from real working people beats the typical business book hands down." – Andrew Ceccon, CMO, OnlineBenefits Inc.

"Books of this publisher are syntheses of actual experiences of real-life, hands-on, front-line leaders—no academic or theoretical nonsense here. Comprehensive, tightly organized, yet nonetheless motivational!" – Lac V. Tran, Senior Vice President, CIO, and Associate Dean, Rush University Medical Center

"Aspatore is unlike other publishers…books feature cutting-edge information provided by top executives working on the front lines of an industry." – Debra Reisenthel, President and CEO, Novasys Medical Inc.

ASPATORE

www.Aspatore.com

Aspatore Books, a Thomson Reuters business, is the largest and most exclusive publisher of C-level executives (CEO, CFO, CTO, CMO, partner) from the world's most respected companies and law firms. Aspatore annually publishes a select group of C-level executives from the Global 1,000, top 250 law firms (partners and chairs), and other leading companies of all sizes. C-Level Business Intelligence™, as conceptualized and developed by Aspatore Books, provides professionals of all levels with proven business intelligence from industry insiders—direct and unfiltered insight from those who know it best—as opposed to third-party accounts offered by unknown authors and analysts. Aspatore Books is committed to publishing an innovative line of business and legal books, those which lay forth principles and offer insights that, when employed, can have a direct financial impact on the reader's business objectives, whatever they may be. In essence, Aspatore publishes critical tools—need-to-read as opposed to nice-to-read books—for all business professionals.

Inside the Minds

The critically acclaimed *Inside the Minds* series provides readers of all levels with proven business intelligence from C-level executives (CEO, CFO, CTO, CMO, partner) from the world's most respected companies. Each chapter is comparable to a white paper or essay and is a future-oriented look at where an industry/profession/topic is heading and the most important issues for future success. Each author has been carefully chosen through an exhaustive selection process by the *Inside the Minds* editorial board to write a chapter for this book. *Inside the Minds* was conceived in order to give readers actual insights into the leading minds of business executives worldwide. Because so few books or other publications are actually written by executives in industry, *Inside the Minds* presents an unprecedented look at various industries and professions never before available.

INSIDE THE MINDS

Employment Dispute Resolution

Leading Lawyers on Examining Company Policies and Procedures, Obtaining Key Information, and Considering Alternative Dispute Resolution

ASPATORE

Mat #40753395

BOOK AND ARTICLE IDEA SUBMISSIONS

If you are a C-level executive, senior lawyer, or venture capitalist interested in submitting a book or article idea to the Aspatore editorial board for review, please e-mail TLR.AspatoreAuthors@thomson.com. Aspatore is especially looking for highly specific ideas that would have a direct financial impact on behalf of a reader. Completed publications can range from 2 to 2,000 pages. Include your book/article idea, biography, and any additional pertinent information.

Inside the Minds Project Manager, Merissa Kraham; edited by Eddie Fournier; proofread by Melanie Zimmerman

---

ISBN 978-0-314-19474-9

For corrections, updates, comments, or any other inquiries, please e-mail TLR.AspatoreEditorial@thomson.com.

First Printing, 2008
10 9 8 7 6 5 4 3 2 1

CONTENTS

The Importance of Knowing Your Clients and Your Facts

Lawrence H. Clore

Partner

Fulbright & Jaworski LLP

ASPATORE

Labor and employment lawyers are responsible for advising their clients on many different issues, including employment discrimination and harassment, wage and hour compliance, occupational safety and health, employment contracts, wage claims, privacy concerns, union organizational efforts, and union negotiations. Indeed, advice is offered on all matters involved in the employer/employee relationship. When disputes regarding these issues mature into litigation, the practice becomes an adversary rather than counseling practice.

Labor and employment attorneys counsel their clients with regard to the legality of personnel actions and represent them against claims of discrimination and harassment. They assist in putting legal policies and procedures into place. They review and audit payroll practices. Employers are represented in inspections by Occupational Safety and Health Administration agents and in resulting litigation. Labor and employment counsel are consulted regarding privacy issues, as well as issues that may result in employees becoming interested in union representation. They defend employers from unfair labor practice cases under the National Labor Relations Act and in representation cases before the National Labor Relations Board and in any resulting relations with labor organizations. Employers are defended against employment tort claims by labor and employment counsel.

It is important that labor and employment lawyers are knowledgeable on all these matters to best serve their clients' needs. For example, a lawyer would not want to create illegal discrimination issues under Title VII of the Civil Rights Act of 1964, as amended, while solving a union problem under the National Labor Relations Act. As Congress enacts further legislation, however, the legal process is becoming increasingly complicated, making it imperative for employment lawyers to stay on top of all developments in the law that affect employers. For example, the Americans with Disabilities Act, the Family Medical Leave Act, and state workers' compensation acts can all apply simultaneously to one situation, such as an employee with an on-the-job injury that constitutes a disability and a serious health condition. In such a situation, three laws with different purposes and objectives collide, creating a scenario where virtually anything an employer does may violate one or more of the statutes.

Strategies to Help Clients

In regards to the workplace, clients tend to make a few key mistakes. First, many clients rely very heavily on their supervisors, without providing sufficient training. In fact, most problems result from poor supervision and communication. Training of supervisors to manage and communicate with their employees and communicate issues to upper management might well put me out of business. I have never seen a problem result from over-trained supervisors.

In the past few years, wage and hour issues have come to the forefront of employment litigation. In fact, filing Fair Labor Standards Act collective actions has become a cottage industry, making a number of attorneys wealthy. To avoid falling victim to this industry, it is important for clients to consistently audit their organization and make sure they are in line with the current federal and state wage and hour laws. A careful review of timekeeping practices, wage payments, and the exempt status of employees can pay real dividends. Training of supervisors on this issue can also be a great help.

Additionally, union activity in Texas and in many other areas has been relatively rare in the past fifteen to twenty years. As a result, supervisors and executives who were well trained and prepared to deal with union organizational activity under the National Labor Relations Act twenty-five to thirty years ago have long since ceased to worry about such activity and no longer assess the effect of the decisions they make on their organization's union vulnerability. It is extremely important that such concerns are revisited and training is implemented to prepare for a new aggressive push by unions into areas once considered geographically safe from union efforts. In addition, new training on dealing with the fairly recent tactic used by unions, commonly called a "corporate campaign," must be undertaken. All this means more training for supervisors and consideration of effects on union vulnerability in connection with every decision made by the client.

Another pitfall for clients is making a decision in haste or anger. Clients often look back with regret on such decisions. It is important for clients to remain level-headed, even in the face of heated and emotional events, and to ensure fair treatment for all involved. There is no guarantee that the outcome will be successful for them. However, treating employees in a way that appears unfair is almost always a guarantee that one's actions will be very hard to defend in subsequent litigation, particularly before a jury. Perception is everything in employee relations.

It is true that the sooner a client recognizes a problem and seeks advice from an employment lawyer, the more successful that client can be in creating a defensible situation. It is the lawyer's job to investigate and resolve the issues in a timely manner. The earlier the problem is resolved, the less expense the client will incur. Often, when problems arise, clients have a natural tendency to ignore them in an effort to avoid trouble and expense. However, ignoring a troublesome situation has the potential to cause it to grow into a larger problem. The most useful piece of advice for clients is to remain on the lookout for problems. When problems do arise, it is important to take action immediately, rather than let the problem fester until it becomes a major challenge. Training your supervisors to report problems quickly to someone who can do something about the problems is, again, invaluable.

Initial Client Meetings: Developing a Strategy

The most important technique to utilize when taking on a new dispute is a thorough investigation. It is imperative that a lawyer know and understand the facts of the case. Only when all the facts have been discovered can the problem be examined and a solution pursued.

When first meeting with a client, it is important to ask a great number of preliminary questions. Often, clients will provide the answers they think are expected or desired of them. It is the lawyer's role to delve deeper into these issues, to determine the key facts of the case. Often, clients will provide a lot of useful information during the questioning period. However, they may leave out a key fact that makes all of their other statements irrelevant. The role of a labor and employment lawyer is to thoroughly investigate all aspects of the case so these key pieces of evidence are not overlooked.

It is also imperative that all documents support the facts of the case. One of the major roles of the client is to assemble all the evidentiary support available that will be useful in the resolution of the case. The principal document to investigate is the personnel file of the employee who is at ground zero of the action. The best approach is for the lawyers to undertake a thorough review of this file in its entirety. If the evidence in the file supports the case and provides useful information, the case may be resolved at trial. However, if the file does not provide any supporting evidence for the case, a quicker resolution may be considered. By investigating and examining the files ahead of time, a lawyer knows whether there is a clear story and whether the employer's files support that story.

Another important area to examine in labor disputes is company policies and procedures. By and large, company policies and procedures are extremely important and are present nearly 80 percent of the time. However, a large problem lies not in the presence of these policies, but in their application. A company can draft a great policy, but it also must live with the restrictions put in place by this policy. The most common example is a no-solicitation policy stating that employees are not to solicit other employees during the time they are to be working. This is an extremely useful policy, especially during a union organizational campaign. However, often a company will bend this rule for organizations such as the United Way or a Little League baseball candy sale. If the policy is not enforced in a number of such instances, then enforcement against union solicitations becomes an unlawful discriminatory enforcement of the policy in violation of the National Labor Relations Act. When a company is deciding whether to adopt a policy, it should first examine its commitment to uniform enforcement of the policy. If there is a lack of will to consistently enforce the policy, it should not be adopted.

Difficulties in Employment Disputes

In the scope of employment disputes, several circumstances are more difficult for lawyers to resolve than others are. For example, in hard economic times for a business, there may be a lack of money to fund pay increases and employee benefits. In view of these conditions, negotiations between unions and companies may become increasingly difficult, particularly if the employees do not believe times are bad. Also, an organization facing its first charge of discrimination is a more difficult client to serve. Organizations finding themselves in a discrimination dispute for the first time often feel as though they have done nothing to warrant being in such a position. Often these employers are seeking vindication rather than resolution. These companies do not come easy to the resolution process, and they are often much more hesitant to settle outside of court. While it is ultimately the client's decision as to how far to pursue the case, economically it often becomes a very questionable proposition. Vindication, if possible at all, is decidedly more expensive than resolution. In such a situation, it is very difficult to serve the client's best interest, particularly since pointing out the economic realities of the situation may sound to the client like a lawyer unwilling to fight for the client. Lawyers must walk a fine line, ensuring they do not appear unwilling to fight for their clients, while trying to guide the client around foolish choices.

However, ultimately it is the client's decision and the client's money when it comes down to a financial issue. If a lawyer can highlight the financial implications of preparing for trial, the clients are often much more willing to consider settlement. This, however, is not an easy feat, and lawyers must approach the situation with great care. Assume, for instance, that legal fees for handling the case through trial will be at least $100,000, and assume the plaintiff's demand is $20,000. The choice is (a) the client can pay me $100,000 and hope to win, with no guarantee, or (b) it can pay the plaintiff $20,000 or less (assuming the plaintiff is willing to negotiate a smaller settlement) and have the case finished. I know what I would choose if it was my money, but I am always surprised by the reaction of some clients. Particularly puzzling are those who desire to spend $80,000 defending the case and then settle for the original demand of $20,000.

Another common obstacle in employment dispute resolution occurs when one or both parties put an unusually high value on the employer/employee relationship. If an employee is out for blood and not money, it becomes difficult to soothe their ego by the payment of money without vindication. By the same token, if the employee simply loves the employer and their job, that can present a hurdle as well. In such cases, the use of an experienced mediator is very helpful to bring a taste of reality to the employee. Experienced plaintiffs' counsel can likewise bring such an employee around. An employer who truly does not want the employee back will also be motivated to pay a bit more to ensure it does not happen.

The government is sometimes an obstacle to reasonable settlement of a case. If the government is in the case, they may claim the public interest demands that the settlement include things the parties do not want in their settlement. One common example is a situation where a government agency, such as the Equal Employment Opportunity Commission that enforces Title VII of the Civil Rights Act of 1964, wants the settlement publicized for its own purposes. This can derail a settlement already agreed to by the private parties. Another example occurs when the agency wants a court decision for its precedential value rather than a settlement favorable to the private plaintiff. In some cases, the presence of a labor union can involve an interest different from the private employee's interest and make settlement difficult or impossible. There are a variety of difficulties that arise in employment disputes. Being a successful labor and employment lawyer requires the use of appropriate strategies to overcome such obstacles.

Steps in Labor Disputes

There are five main steps in every labor dispute. First, each situation must begin with investigation so the lawyer truly understands the key facts and nature of the case. Next, the uncovered evidence must be held up to the standards of the law. Additionally, the lawyer must examine the other side of the case and the attorney representing the claimant. Third is a further investigation through the history of the supervisor as well as the comparators. It is especially important to determine what the weaknesses of the case are so the lawyer is prepared to handle inquiries from the opposing side. It is a litigator's job to ensure he or she understands the weaknesses of their case better than the other side does. The fourth stage is either fighting or negotiating oneself out of a fight. In reality, an objective of the combat is to ensure the case is in such a posture that, if negotiations do occur, the client will be on favorable ground for the fifth stage. The last or fifth stage is the actual resolution. Whether it is through trial or settlement, it is important for a lawyer to know how to approach each situation to achieve resolution.

It is very difficult to know how long each successive step will take, as there are many unknowns when dealing with employment disputes. In many instances, it falls within the client's control to some extent. By way of example, if the client expresses a desire to settle, there is no need to spend one to two years and a great sum of money reaching the point of settlement. However, the stages of an employment dispute cannot be completely controlled by the attorney. Often, clients do not respond to reasonable offers. In these instances, it is the lawyer's role to be mindful of the ultimate direction of the case and be careful not to spend money on issues that are not absolutely necessary to the successful conclusion of the case.

When working with regular clients, a lawyer can predict, with some degree of certainty, what to anticipate in terms of client expectations. With new clients, however, it is somewhat more difficult to gauge their expectations. The lawyer's role is to be as candid and up front as possible, especially when laying out the realities of the situation. Additionally, it is necessary for the lawyer and client to develop a relationship so each understands the other's expectations regarding the case. Establishing a relationship in which the lawyer and client can discuss the constraints and opportunities of each situation is imperative to achieving a successful outcome.

Alternatives in Resolution Outcomes

There are a variety of alternative resolutions available for employment disputes. Mediation, for one, is a very useful resource and has been effective for a number of years. In fact, many mediators claim to resolve more than 95 percent of their cases. More than twenty years ago, the Equal Employment Opportunity Commission established a process known as the "fact-finding conference." These conferences were not intended to be mediations, but they were similar in terms of their structure. Each conference required an employer and employee and their respective counsels, as well as an Equal Employment Opportunity Commission investigator, to be present in one small room. First, the charging party would explain their claim without interruption. Then the employer would explain their position without interruption. Many times, it was clear this was the first time the two parties had communicated effectively with each other. During many conferences, the parties discovered the dispute was really a failure of communication, and many such charges were resolved on the spot.

Civil rights groups, however, did not like these conferences and finally put an end to them. These groups felt the claims made by employees were being overlooked and trivialized. No huge changes or great sums of money were made because of these conferences. The net result was just that disputes were being resolved amicably. Mediations, while similar to fact-finding conferences, are more formal and much more expensive. However, the net effect is the same and, statistically, the results are even better. From a lawyer's perspective, mediation is a useful approach to resolving disputes, as well as a much less costly alternative to a trial.

A good financial outcome is achieved when the client is happy. However, making the client happy is not an easy task, as clients have different desires in the resolution of their cases than lawyers do. Communication between a lawyer and client is essential to determine what is expected from each side. Lawyers always consider a win in trial the highest form of success, as it not only pays the bills, but it builds credibility and a strong reputation as well. However, if every case is handled in such a manner, chances are the lawyer's client pool will begin to diminish. While clients love to win, the reality of the situation is that many cannot afford to win and certainly cannot afford the cost of victory very often. Success in a case requires an understanding of one's clients and the ability to balance individual goals.

The Rise in International Disputes

There is an increasing trend today toward disputes involving international clients, whether it is regarding employees moving to a foreign country to continue operations or employing those already residing in foreign countries. In such instances, it is recommended and almost always necessary to contact a lawyer in the appropriate country. Each nation has its own laws and approach to employment law. Therefore, it is unlikely that a lawyer from another country will be competent in all the necessary areas to achieve success for their client.

One of the greatest challenges in foreign employment that clients face pertains to U.S. employers sending workers to foreign countries that may not be stable, either from a security or political standpoint. In these instances, lawyers can protect the clients as best as they can under American law and the laws of the state where they are employed. In terms of employing a foreign national in that foreign country, however, it is most effective for clients to be directed to an attorney in that country. Essentially, the laws and regulations vary so much from country to country that employing an appropriate attorney in the applicable country is the most reasonable course of action.

Lawrence H. Clore has been a partner in Fulbright & Jaworski LLP's labor and employment law section in the firm's Houston office since 1977. He has been continuously engaged in representing management in all types of labor and employment law matters, including litigation under federal and state statutes regulating employment, litigation of miscellaneous employment torts, representation of employers before state and federal administrative agencies regulating employment and labor matters, and counseling employers with regard to such matters since 1971. In addition, he has handled numerous traditional labor law matters, including contract negotiations with unions and elections under the National Labor Relations Act. He has particularly extensive experience in the health care industry, and has had substantial experience in the construction, retail, funeral, financial services, petroleum, and manufacturing industries.

Mr. Clore is certified in labor and employment law by the Texas Board of Legal Specialization. He is a past chairman of the labor and employment law section of the State Bar of Texas and the Houston Management Lawyer's Forum. He is also a member of the American Bar Association's section on labor and employment law. He is included in Who's Who in American Law *and* The Best Lawyers in America. *He was named a "Texas Super Lawyer" in labor and employment law in the November 2003 issue of* Texas Monthly.

Mr. Clore received a B.B.A. with a concentration in industrial relations and personnel management from Texas Christian University, and a J.D. with honors from the University of Texas School of Law. While in law school, he was an editor of the Texas Law Review *and a member of Chancellors and the Order of the Coif. Following his graduation from law school, he served two years in the U.S. Army Medical Services Corps. He was admitted to practice law in Texas in 1969 and in various federal courts in 1972.*

Establishing and Achieving the Client's Goals

William M. Betley

Partner

Atkinson, Andelson, Loya, Ruud & Romo

ASPATORE

The general approach in every new employment dispute should be to immediately communicate with the client and determine, initially, how the client views the case and would like to have the dispute handled. Because employment matters are often very emotional, due to their very personal nature, it is extremely important at the outset to determine the position of the client so counsel will be better able to provide advice and develop a viable strategy.

Loss Prevention

Because I exclusively represent employers, my initial focus in employment issues is always on loss prevention. In that role, I regularly review company handbooks, policies and procedures, applications, company-sponsored orientation and mentoring programs, and any wage and hour documents and/or bonus program that could result in an employment dispute or lawsuit. My review of these materials is meant to ensure my client is in full compliance with all applicable labor laws and that any inconsistencies or ambiguities in those policies and procedures are clarified and corrected.

Additionally, as part of my loss prevention review, I regularly interface with human resources personnel and company managers and supervisors to ensure understanding, adherence, and compliance with the company policies and procedures. I also will visit my client's facility or place of business to observe how the various policies are being implemented.

Again, my primary focus at this stage is loss prevention. Through a concerted effort of regular document and policy review, communication with client decision-makers, and having a detailed understanding of my client's operation, I am generally able to accomplish that goal.

Employment Dispute: Initial Steps

Unfortunately, employment disputes and resulting lawsuits do occasionally occur. The issues involved in those disputes, from discrimination, unlawful harassment, and wrongful termination to wage and hour issues, workplace injuries, and benefits questions, are usually very emotional matters, making resolution challenging.

Certainly, at the outset of any employment dispute, I again review relevant company policies and procedures to ensure they comply with current law. I then again conduct an exhaustive review of relevant managers and supervisors to ensure that company policies and procedures have been stringently understood and followed.

Documentation is particularly important, from a defense prospective, in defending employment lawsuits. Examples of potentially helpful documentation include well-reasoned employee performance reviews, disciplinary or performance-related write-ups, employee critiques and/or evaluations prepared by managers and supervisors, signed acknowledgements to any employee handbooks and/or relevant company policies, or any other document related to the employment dispute.

The initial review of relevant documents will often determine the strengths and/or weaknesses of a party's position. If, for example, the reviewed company policy dealing with sexual harassment is thorough, well written, and complies with existing labor laws, the initial element in providing an effective and persuasive defense is met. If, on the other hand, that policy is either outdated or nonexistent, the defense of the employer becomes much more problematic and could result in the immediate exploration of dispute resolution.

Once relevant documents have been reviewed and found to comply with relevant labor laws, the next step is to ensure those policies have been understood and adhered to by company employees. Detailed interviews of company managers and supervisors is necessary to ascertain their understanding of those policies and procedures, how they typically implement those policies and procedures, and how those policies and procedures were implemented in the current dispute. At this stage, it is also important to determine how credible those managers and supervisors will be when testifying in deposition, arbitration, or trial.

Often, there is a disconnect between the actual policy and the manager's understanding of that policy, resulting in an improper or incorrect implementation.

After this initial analysis, it is then necessary to again discuss the matter with the employer's ultimate decision-maker and re-evaluate the employment dispute in order to better assess the probability of success and establish a defense strategy on an ongoing basis.

Because, as mentioned earlier, employment cases are very emotional, one of the greatest challenges in discussing strategy and/or resolution is separating the emotions involved in the dispute from the actual merits. The emotional component in employment cases cannot be overstated and is often as important in the overall handling of these cases as are the allegations themselves.

Difficult Disputes to Resolve

Generally, because employment disputes tend to be personal in nature, they are, as a whole, difficult to resolve. Typically, wage and hour issues, namely disputes over employee classification, overtime payments, benefits, or salary disputes, are easier to resolve because of the objective nature of those disputes. In those cases, a specific labor law can be objectively applied to the dispute to establish not only liability, but also a calculation of damages, including any penalties and/or interest.

Overtime disputes usually become a mathematical calculation. Employee classification issues typically revolve around job descriptions and related responsibilities. Employee benefits usually revert to company documents and corresponding labor law provisions. Those matters, while emotional, can be dealt with in a fairly objective manner.

Disputes dealing with issues of discrimination, wrongful termination, and unlawful harassment are often the most difficult to resolve because they are much more subjective in nature. They often stem from an unwelcome physical touching or a degrading comment or expletive. Although there are specific statutes and policies relevant to those issues, the ultimate determination and eventual calculation of damages is much more subjective in nature. Those disputes often hinge on credibility issues and often result in the creation of workplace cliques or factions, inasmuch as the resolution of those disputes is often based on corroborating information or testimony.

Even in instances where liability is established, the question of damages is often uncertain and is based, in large measure, on nothing more than the pre.sentation of evidence and the likeability of the employee versus the employer. If an employee believes he or she has been discriminated against, sexually harassed, or wrongfully terminated, or, conversely, if the employer believes no sexual harassment has been perpetrated or that the policies against sexual harassment were not strictly followed by the employee, or that there was no discrimination, or that the termination of the employee was justified, those positions will result in a stalemate, making a mediated resolution very difficult

Alternative Dispute Resolution

Pre-litigation dispute resolution solely between the parties should always be encouraged. In that setting, face-to-face contact between the parties, without representation and without mediation, is preferred. This type of meeting creates a more informal setting that is less adversarial and intimidating. The goal of this session is to resolve the dispute, but if that is not possible, to at least allow both sides to present their respective positions without the presence of advocates. This initial meeting sets the tone for continued dialogue and makes a later joint session in a more formal mediation setting much easier and more productive.

Often, the determining factor of whether an employee decides to litigate depends on how the employer initially responded to the dispute. Certainly, a willingness on the part of the employer to conduct an investigation and engage in dialogue aimed at resolving the dispute demonstrates the seriousness with which the employer views that claim. The decision to litigate a claim against an employer often stems from the employee's feeling of a lack of respect by the employer concerning the claim.

An overt lack of respect resulting in complete inaction (or worse, retaliation against an employee for bringing his or her claim) is almost certain to escalate an internal employment dispute into a litigated case. Employers would be wise to seriously investigate all employment disputes, never retaliate against an employee for bringing a claim, and attempt to resolve the dispute in-house as expeditiously as possible. In situations in which a case cannot be informally resolved internally, consideration should be made toward the utilization of a trained mediator. Because of the cost involved in retaining an effective mediator, timing is particularly important with respect to the retention of his or her services.

Depending on the motivation of the respective sides, a mediator should be retained after formal litigation has ensued and after sufficient discovery has been conducted to allow both sides to have a full and complete understanding of the strengths and weaknesses of their case. Conversely, the mediation should be scheduled before extensive litigation expenses, expert review, and trial preparation have ensued to make the mediator's eventual cost/benefit analysis argument feasible.

In those cases in which the emotions overcome the pragmatic approach to dispute resolution, expenses will often exceed the value of the case because of the unreasonable position of the parties. These cases are often doomed to proceed to trial.

As important as the timing of the mediation is the actual selection of the mediator. Because employment disputes are unique, any mediator selected should be a specialist in the area and have experience in the specific issues in controversy. Retaining the services of a mediator without the requisite experience can often lead to frustration, since the parties will not feel that their positions are being understood and that they are not getting sufficient return on the selection of a mediator. An inexperienced mediator can also lose control of the mediation, resulting in the parties' emotions dominating the proceedings rather than common sense and pragmatism.

Mediators, specializing in employment law, are not inexpensive. However, the experience provided by a qualified employment mediator will prove invaluable when discussing issues as diverse as applicable policies and procedures, relevant case and statutory authority, liability analysis, case value, jury appeal, and future litigation costs. The experienced employment mediator has the credibility to address all of the issues, and ultimately it will be that credibility and his or her persuasiveness that will determine whether the dispute is settled at the mediation stage or the litigation continues.

Arbitration

If the matter does not settle at the mediation stage, turning to binding arbitration is often the most effective and expeditious way of resolving the employment dispute. The unique nature of employment cases not only creates unique challenges during the investigation, discovery, and mediation phases, but also during the litigation and trial phases.

Because issues are often raised in employment matters that are foreign to civil court judges and difficult to objectively grasp for typical juries, the utilization of an arbitrator affords both sides the best opportunity for a reasoned, rational result. Whereas a judge in either a state or federal court is randomly selected, the parties choosing arbitration are able to review the qualifications of various arbitrators and mutually agree to their selection. Those arbitrators are experienced in the employment issues before them, and they are much better equipped to review the evidence in a rational manner than an inexperienced jury is. Also, the utilization of the arbitration process ensures the parties of a date certain by which the matter will be decided. Given today's court backlog, it often takes as long as five years for a matter to reach trial from the date the complaint is filed.

The parties in an arbitration are basically able to establish a reasonable schedule, conduct necessary discovery, and present evidence to the arbitrator, as the trier of fact, as if the matter were being tried before a judge.

The benefits to arbitration over trial are numerous. Those advantages include a much more expeditious conclusion, a fairly economical litigation process, the ability to present the case in front of an individual who is well versed in the issues in controversy, and the somewhat more relaxed atmosphere of the arbitration setting.

Disadvantages to the utilization of arbitration include the obligation of the employer to bear the entire expense of the arbitrator, which can be a significant consideration. Also, in arbitrations, the ability to dispose of the matter through summary judgment is usually not available to either side. Last, there are almost no opportunities to appeal a binding arbitration decision. Both parties generally must accept the judgment of the arbitrator as final. Despite these disadvantages, the utilization of the arbitration process is more desirable than the utilization of the court system.

Litigation Budget

Obviously, economics are an important consideration in resolving employment disputes. The best way to curb overzealous emotionalism and place a more pragmatic approach on the handling of employment disputes is the preparation of the litigation budget. Multiple litigation budgets should be prepared throughout the course of the employment dispute and resulting litigation to provide the client with a clear cost/benefit analysis.

An initial litigation budget should be contemplated through the preparation for a motion for summary judgment. Included in that initial litigation budget should be the hard costs incurred for the filing of all pleadings, the cost for various deposition transcripts, any expert costs that might be incurred prior to the preparation for summary judgment, any mediation costs, and any anticipated copying or other related costs. In addition to these hard costs, a realistic billable time estimate should be provided by the attorney to provide the client with an accurate picture of anticipated legal fees and costs through the preparation of the motion for summary judgment.

As the matter evolves and circumstances change, modified litigation budgets should be prepared and submitted. After the motion for summary judgment is concluded, another litigation budget should be prepared, anticipating legal fees and costs through trial. As with the prior litigation budget, all anticipated hard costs should be included. Additionally, in this litigation budget, the length of trial should be anticipated and additional issues such as paralegal utilization, additional manpower costs, preparation of trial exhibits, and travel expenses of experts and/or witnesses should be included.

In the area of dispute resolution, the main function of the litigation budget is to provide the client with the anticipated costs of either prosecuting or defending the matter. Such an analysis often assists the client in making the often painstaking decision of whether to resolve the dispute or continue with the litigation with the uncertain result.

Often, once a verdict is rendered, the opportunity for case resolution still exists. Therefore, it is necessary to provide the client with a third litigation budget, post-trial, which will contemplate any appellate issues and costs.

Again, this third budget will allow the client to make a rational decision of how best to proceed with respect to matter resolution.

Obviously, because of the emotional nature of employment disputes, the preparation of litigation budgets at the earliest opportunity are important tools to assist both the client and his or her representative in reaching a decision based on the realities of the dispute and the costs involved in either presenting or defending those issues, as opposed to the raw emotions often at the forefront of these cases. Well-prepared, well-thought-out litigation budgets are an invaluable tool.

Establishing a Successful Client Relationship

Getting the client invested in the dispute and/or litigation is the best way of establishing a successful client relationship. This is accomplished by candidly discussing the facts of the dispute with the client and asking the client to provide you with his or her desired goals to be accomplished. This conversation often establishes a baseline from which the attorney/client relationship can evolve.

Certainly, the attorney must be candid and honest in his or her assessment of the case, being sensitive to the proposed goals established by the client. It is vital that the attorney be able to support his or her conclusions and recommendations, and that his or her knowledge of the facts of the dispute be complete. It is necessary that the client consider his or her attorney part of the team, and that the effort will be collective and decisions will be made through collaborative input. All significant decisions must include input from the client, and direct communication should take place as often as practicable.

Certainly given today's technology, e-mails, cell phone communication, and text messaging should be part of the normal communication between attorney and client.

By thoroughly understanding every aspect of the employment dispute, demonstrating a command of the issues and corresponding law, establishing a commitment to the team concept, investing the client in the decision-making and eventual outcome, and frequently and regularly communicating with the client, an excellent attorney/client relationship can be forged.

William M. Betley practices in all areas of employment law, including unlawful harassment, discrimination, wrongful termination, employee classification, and wage and hour issues. He also counsels and represents architects, engineers, and subcontractors in all phases of construction planning, development, negotiation, and litigation.

Mr. Betley is a frequent speaker on numerous employment issues such as unlawful harassment, disability discrimination, leaves of absence, workplace violence, employment handbooks, and hiring and firing issues. He is also the chairman of the Inland Valleys Employer Advisory Council, and he is the editor of that organization's employment newsletter.

Mr. Betley was admitted to practice law in California in 1984. He is a member of the American Bar Association, the Defense Research Institute, the Inland Valleys Employer Advisory Council, the Orange County Employer Advisory Council, the California Chamber of Commerce, the Society for Human Resources Management, the Professionals in Human Resources Association, the Orange County Bar Association, the Building Industry Association, and the Home Builders Council. He is listed in the National Registry of Who's Who for Attorneys in the United States.

Addressing Labor and Employment Disputes: Considering All the Circumstances

Chris Baker

Partner

Thelen Reid Brown Raysman & Steiner LLP

ASPATORE

Determining the best approach to resolving a labor or employment dispute depends significantly on when, how, and why the dispute arose, as well as the client's wishes.[1] There is no generic or boilerplate approach. For example, if a dispute with an employee arises in the workplace, with the employee still performing their job well, that is a very different situation from one in which an employee starts raising claims because they think they are about to be fired. And those situations are obviously different from a labor dispute where a union is threatening to strike, or a situation where a lawsuit has been filed or an employer has received a demand letter from a terminated employee's counsel. Each dispute is unique in its own way, and each has to be taken on its own terms. Determining the best way to resolve a dispute means, initially, understanding what the dispute is about and, probably most importantly, determining what your client seeks in the way of an outcome.

Researching a Labor Dispute

The first thing I do when asked to handle a labor and employment dispute is to find out what the client wants to achieve. I also try to determine what the client would consider a "win," given the situation. I attempt to drill down a little in determining a client's objectives because sometimes the client hasn't fully thought through what it would like to have happen. Also, sometimes the client's initial expectations are not entirely realistic given the state of the law. For example, say an employee files a non-frivolous discrimination lawsuit. What the employer may initially consider a win would be that the employee's case is dismissed the following week and the employee pays all of the employer's attorneys' fees, and perhaps some sort of damages as well. This is an extreme (and somewhat fanciful) example, but it gives you the idea. In determining a client's objectives, I also discuss its expectations. Sometimes an attorney has to let the client know what is possible, what is likely, and what is not.

Next, I conduct an investigation. If it is an employment dispute, I may talk to managers and other employees about their interactions with the

[1] "Labor and employment law" usually encompasses both "traditional labor law" (meaning, basically, the laws governing the relationship between employers and unions) and "employment law" (meaning, basically, all the laws governing the relationship between an employer and its employees directly).

employee at the center of the dispute. I may also review pertinent employment contracts and handbooks, and other background documents. If it is a discrimination or harassment case, it is important to ensure that the client has a good anti-discrimination policy, because that is a document a company will rely on heavily if the case goes to trial. Some employer handbooks also call for mediation prior to an employee filing a claim, and in appropriate circumstances, an employer may want to take advantage of an early mediation. I will also review documents that are relevant to the dispute. For example, if an employee has a claim that someone sent him or her sexually explicit e-mails, I will obviously review these e-mails.

If it is a wage and hour dispute, I will review and analyze the company's pay practices. Understanding the client's pay procedures and policies is incredibly important in the wage and hour context. Some wage and hour cases are of the "gotcha" variety, meaning the employer has a standard policy that, often for technical reasons, does not comply with the law. Understanding the potential exposure as early in the case as possible is important in determining how best to achieve a resolution at an optimal price.

Finally, I will usually research the employee's attorney to determine his or her reputation, and whether he or she is pragmatic or a "true believer." The quality of an employee's attorney can tell one a lot about the potential value and potential cost of a case. The good plaintiffs' attorneys usually don't file lousy cases. They do their own investigation and draw their own conclusions before taking on the representation. Moreover, unless there is a significant fact of which they are unaware, the good plaintiffs' counsel generally will not go away for a song, even if the case turns out to be not nearly as strong as they initially believed. But they do tend to be rational, and a fair or reasonable resolution can be achieved.

All of this is essentially an information-gathering exercise to determine the best way to approach and, hopefully, resolve the dispute.

Difficult Disputes: Successful Strategies

A number of very different variables can affect how easy or hard it is to resolve a dispute. These variables include: if the employee, in their heart of hearts, feels they have been "wronged" if an employee has an emotional investment in the litigation itself, if the employee's attorney can't control their client, if the employee's attorney's ego is larger than the real value of the case, if the employer believes an important principle is at stake, if the lawsuit seeks to change how the employer does business, and of course, how much money is at stake.

With that said, the employment disputes that probably require the lightest touch are those where the employee in question is a current (not former) employee. This is because any adverse act by the employer against a current employee could lead to a retaliation claim. Also, there may be political considerations that need to be taken into account (if the employee is protected by one manager but not another). And on occasion, there may be potential workplace violence issues if the dispute involves a very volatile employee.

One strategy I might employ with an employee who is still in the workplace involves figuring out a way to reduce the emotional level of the dispute. If a dispute has reached the point where a lawyer is involved, it is likely that the employee is going to eventually leave the workplace because their presence is having a detrimental impact (and the employee usually doesn't want to be there anymore anyway). Thus, the employee's resignation usually becomes a deal point in resolving the controversy. Finally, in these kinds of disputes, it is important to recognize that the attorney initially handling the dispute for the employer might be conflicted out of any subsequent litigation because, as the attorney, he or she may be a witness in the case (e.g., if the attorney is asked by the employer to interview witnesses or prepare a harassment report).

In cases involving high levels of emotion (where, for example, an angry former employee has brought suit), it is good for everyone to recognize that resolving the dispute may take time. You may have to engage in discovery and motion practice and allow the wheels of justice to turn in their slow but inevitable way. Eventually both the employer and employee may begin to see the value of a settlement. The employer may move from a mindset of "millions for defense, but not one cent for tribute" to a mindset of "we need to move on." The employee may find a new job, or have strained financial resources, or finally recognize the toll the litigation is taking on their life, and decide a resolution is in their best interests.

Once the parties and their attorneys recognize the value of resolution, the process becomes easier. The first step is getting everyone on the boat (meaning everyone agrees a resolution is best). The second step is rowing the boat to shore (actually getting the deal done). Getting people on the boat usually takes more creativity and energy than getting the deal done. Sometimes the attorneys will think the employee is on board, only to find out later that he or she isn't really, and is now looking for ways to blow up the deal.

Important State and Federal Laws and Landmark Cases

The laws that probably give rise to the most employment litigation are those that limit an employer's ability to terminate (or refuse to hire or reinstate) an employee. These include the anti-discrimination and harassment laws (e.g., Title VII, the Americans with Disabilities Act, the Age Discrimination in Employment Act, etc.), leave laws (e.g., the Family and Medical Leave Act, the Uniformed Services Employment and Reemployment Act, etc.), and various laws prohibiting adverse action against whistleblowers (e.g., the False Claims Act, Sarbanes-Oxley, etc.).

In addition, wage and hour laws are now a major focus of both plaintiff and defense attorneys. This is because the violation of wage and hour laws can often give rise to class action claims, which are much more profitable for plaintiffs' attorneys. Wage and hour claims include those pertaining to the misclassification of employees, failure to allow meal or rest breaks, the improper calculation of regular rate of pay, the failure to reimburse expenses, and the list goes on and on. Most of these claims are brought under the state law equivalents of the Fair Labor Standards Act. Cases are also being brought these days under the Fair Labor Standards Act, though not as many because employees must "opt in" to Fair Labor Standards Act collective actions, whereas employees must generally "opt out" of state law class actions.

Consistent with the bar's recent emphasis of wage and hour law, recent important cases in labor and employment law have focused on compensation issues. Generally, they have reached conclusions that have benefited employees. For example, in *Murphy v. Kenneth Cole Productions*, the California Supreme Court determined that a claim alleging a violation of California's meal and rest break laws has a four-year statute of limitations instead of a one-year statute, which means these types of cases are four times more profitable for plaintiffs' attorneys and the employees they represent than they otherwise would have been. Similarly, in *Gentry v. Superior Court*, the California Supreme Court discouraged the use of class action waivers in employment arbitration agreements, finding that, while such waivers are not necessarily unenforceable, an employer has a high burden to prove they are. Lastly, in *Gattuso v. Hart-Hank Shoppers*, the court determined that, while an employer could reimburse its employees' expenses through an increased wage, it had to separate out which part of the compensation was for expense reimbursements and which part was for the employee's labor. As wage and hour cases continue to be a favorite among plaintiffs' counsel, I expect the courts to continue to issue significant decisions in this area.

Finally, another important set of laws are those that establish an employer's obligations when shutting down a plant or laying off employees. These include the notice and severance obligations set forth in the Worker Adjustment and Retraining Notification Act, the notice obligations set forth in the Older Workers Benefit Protection Act, and an employer's obligation to engage in "effects bargaining" with a union when winding down operations. A plant closure can give rise to numerous employment disputes, and attention to detail is a must. (See the checklist attached as Appendix A for a description of the items an employer should consider when closing a plant or engaging in a mass layoff.)

Interpreting Labor Law: Be Pragmatic

Many labor and employment laws are based on simple, easy-to-understand concepts. For example, the law against gender discrimination means you cannot discriminate against a woman because she is a woman. There are only so many fine points you can attach to this basic proposition. Indeed, if you get too hung up on the ultra-fine points of employment law, especially in a termination case, you may be doing the client a disservice.

For example, in handling an employment termination case, there are two big strategic questions. First, can you defeat the case on summary judgment? And second, what is the jury going to think about this set of facts, regardless of what the law may provide? Because it is sometimes difficult to defeat an employment termination case on summary judgment (there are often disputed material facts), an employment attorney needs to be thinking about how a jury is going to view the facts of the dispute early on. For example, although one may be tempted to tell the client, "I think you have a good defense in this harassment case, because the harasser in your workforce harassed everyone, not just women, and thus he wasn't really engaged in *gender* harassment but rather undifferentiated harassment," this may not be the best defense to put forward at trial. Indeed, paying too much attention to the fine points of the law can ultimately create client management issues, because the fine points (especially in termination cases) do not necessarily rule the day in the labor and employment context where a jury will likely be inclined to mete out rough justice regardless of legal niceties.

Recent Labor Law Resolution Trends

As the cost of litigation has increased, litigants have searched for less expensive means of dispute resolution. The most popular form currently is mediation. Indeed, mediation—where a mediator tries to facilitate an informal resolution of the case—has now replaced trial as the primary form of dispute resolution.

Arbitration—where an arbitrator decides the case, usually after a hearing—is another popular form of dispute resolution. Labor arbitration in the union context has been around for a long time. Employers and unions also use adjustment boards to resolve employee grievances early in the process. In the non-union context, employment arbitration has definitely become much more popular over the last ten years or so. However, because of court restrictions on the content of arbitration agreements, employment arbitration is now often just as expensive as the court system. (See Appendix B for a sample arbitration agreement incorporating these restrictions.) Because of this, and because arbitration decisions are typically not subject to appeal, some employers are backing off a bit from insisting on the arbitration of employment disputes as a condition of an employee's employment.

Labor and Employment Dispute Resolution

Once a complaint is filed in a labor and employment dispute, one needs to determine whether it is likely that the case will take some time to resolve—

and this determination will depend on the type of dispute one is dealing with. If you believe the dispute is not the type that will take a lot of time to resolve, largely because there are not a lot of emotions or money involved, I would recommend reaching out to the plaintiff's counsel to get an early sense of the settlement value the plaintiff attaches to the case. In a larger lawsuit, you may have to take a harder line before you start talking about mediation or settlement.

One of the primary financial considerations in a run-of-the-mill employment dispute is the cost of defense. Indeed, in many employment disputes the cost of defense is greater than the settlement value or the amount to which the employee should be entitled, and because of the high cost of attorneys' fees, clients often end up settling non-meritorious cases.

In the larger cases (such as class actions), the cost of defense matters less. What matters more may be the discount the client is obtaining on potential liability. Thus, it is important for the client to assess and understand their true potential liability as early in the case as possible. In wage and hour cases, this is usually possible because much of the data should already be available to the employer.

With respect to union disputes, any cost analysis must include how much "pain" the union can inflict on the employer's operations. Can the employer handle the costs of a strike or sabotage? Is it willing to use replacement workers? If there is a strike, how long will it be before the union will be willing to come to the table? What are the public relations issues that may influence the employer? An employer's pain threshold in some ways dictates how hard it can bargain for the underlying collective bargaining agreement.

A good financial outcome in a labor and employment dispute will depend on the nature of the suit. For example, if I represented a client in a wage and hour dispute with $30 million worth of exposure, and I have settled that lawsuit for pennies on the dollar, that might be a great outcome. On the other hand, if I settle a case worth $50,000 for $100,000, that might not seem like a good outcome at first glance. However, if a trial would have embarrassed the company, cost the company significantly more in attorneys' fees, or distracted important executives, the outcome might be entirely justifiable. In the employment context, short-term financial considerations do not always rule the day. An employer might have a very good reason for paying a premium to resolve a particular dispute.

The Client/Attorney Relationship

The key element of a positive client/attorney relationship in this practice area is communication. I tend to err on the side of too much communication rather than too little. This gives me the ability to get a sense as to what the client really cares about and what is less important to them with respect to the progress of the litigation. I always keep the client in the loop on the material aspects of the case, because a client should never be surprised by anything that happens during the course of litigation. In many respects, the most important parts of my job are both zealously advocating on their behalf and managing their expectations so they can perform their own risk analysis. With respect to what I ask of my clients, I ask that they never lie to me, and that they produce documents, witnesses, and information on a timely basis so I do not lose credibility with the court or the other party.

Fortunately, my clients tend to be sophisticated, and they know what is important in the litigation process. I also have some smaller clients, and the litigation process can be new and scary to them. These clients need, deserve, and receive additional support and hand-holding. There is a big difference between representing a Fortune 100 company and representing a family-owned restaurant.

With respect to international clients, they tend to be familiar with the complex nature of labor and employment laws in general. However, they may not be familiar with the exposure that attaches to those laws in the United States. For example, the at-will doctrine of employment is significantly limited in many European countries. Accordingly, European employers will expect to pay some sort of severance when discharging an employee. What they do not always expect, however, is a lawsuit alleging discrimination in which the plaintiff counsel calls them racist or sexist and the plaintiff's counsel demands $1 million.

Developing a Timetable

In some cases, the court will develop a dispute resolution/negotiation timetable for you. In other cases, you have to look at outside considerations. For example, if you are in negotiations with a union for a project labor agreement and you represent the contractor, the negotiation timetable will be governed by when you have to start construction and when you have to be done. In other cases, the timetable for litigation or negotiations is driven by the type of case you have, and the types of personalities you are dealing with. Sometimes you need a long timetable to allow everyone to cool down and understand they are in for a fight. In other cases, the dispute can be resolved quickly, prior to even filing a responsive pleading in court.

Final Advice

The most important piece of advice I could give to another labor attorney is to make sure to really know and understand his or her clients. As a labor and employment attorney, you are a counselor as well as an advocate. Do not ever forget the "counselor's" part of your job.

Chris Baker is a partner with Thelen Reid Brown Raysman & Steiner LLP. He focuses on the representation of a wide array of clients, ranging from Internet start-ups to multinational companies, on all labor and employment matters. He has first chair litigation and trial experience before federal and state courts, the National Labor Relations Board, the Cal-OSHA Appeals Board, and other state agencies, as well as arbitration proceedings. He also has white collar experience representing employers and targeted employees in criminal cases, extensive experience representing and advising employers on Occupational Safety and Health Administration matters, and extensive experience representing companies in commercial litigation involving Americans with Disabilities Act access, the Unruh Act (anti-discrimination laws), fraud, negligence, breach of contract, and so on.

Mr. Baker earned both his B.A., magna cum laude, and his J.D. from the University of Cincinnati, where he was a member of the editorial board of the Cincinnati Law Review. *He is a member of the San Francisco and California Bar Associations, and he is admitted to practice in California and Ohio, as well as before the U.S. Courts of Appeals for the Sixth, Eighth, Ninth, and District of Columbia Circuits, and the U.S. District Courts of California.*

Employer Strategies for Resolving Sarbanes-Oxley Whistleblower Claims

Allegra Lawrence-Hardy

Partner

Sutherland Asbill & Brennan LLP

ASPATORE

Workplace retaliation claims pose significant concerns for employers, both because these cases are so difficult to resolve prior to trial and because there are just so many of them. Now, in addition to retaliation claims based on employment discrimination statutes, publicly traded companies (and certain other employers) also must be prepared to defend against retaliation claims based on the whistleblower provisions enacted as part of the Sarbanes-Oxley Act of 2002 (SOX). 18 U.S.C. §1514A. The SOX whistleblower provision can lead to large damages awards, as in the case of one employer who was recently ordered to pay $642,941 to a successful SOX plaintiff to compensate for "the diminution in expected earnings in all of her future jobs for as long as the reputational injury is expected to affect her prospects." *Hagman v. Washington Mut. Bank*, 2005-SOX-73, at 40 (ALJ December 19, 2006). While SOX retaliation claims have much in common with civil rights retaliation claims, they present other issues employers and their attorneys may not have encountered previously. Because SOX established a unique type of whistleblower protection, steps should be taken to ensure that key members of management are trained on the issues that might arise in this type of retaliation claim.

Unlike most state and federal anti-discrimination statutes, there can be a significant threshold issue as to whether a particular employee is protected by SOX. For example, what if an individual is employed by a non-publicly traded affiliate or subsidiary of a SOX company? What if the individual is an independent contractor providing services to a SOX company? What if the individual works for a SOX company, but resides overseas? The answers to these initial questions will determine whether the employee has the right to bring a SOX whistleblower claim.

For employees of companies subject to SOX, the SOX whistleblower provision allows them to assert a claim if they believe they have been subjected to retaliation because they engaged in "protected" whistleblower activity. SOX prohibits a covered employer from retaliating against an employee because the employee provided information or assisted in an investigation regarding conduct the employee reasonably believed was a violation of specified federal laws and regulations relating to fraud against shareholders. See 18 U.S.C. §1514A(a)(1).

For an employee's activity to be protected by SOX, the employee must (1) reasonably believe the company's conduct violates one of the federal laws and regulations listed in the SOX whistleblower provision, and (2) express concern over the perceived violation. *Henrich v. ECOLAB Inc.*, ARB No. 05-030, ALJ Case No. 2004-SOX-51 (ARB June 29, 2006). "The reported information must have a certain degree of specificity [and] must state particular concerns, which, at the very least, reasonably identify [the company's] conduct that the complainant believes to be illegal." *Bozeman v. Per-Se Technologies*, 456 F. Supp. 2d 1282 (N.D. Ga. 2006). An employee must show that he or she reasonably believed the employer violated (or attempted to violate) one of the federal laws and regulations listed in the SOX whistleblower provision. *Joy v. Robbins & Myers Inc.*, 2007-SOX-74, at **26-27 (ALJ January 30, 2008) (employee failed to establish protected activity where he reported a possible SOX violation that could occur in the future if the employer failed to act). The employee's belief must be reasonably based on the knowledge available to a reasonable person in the same factual circumstances and with the same training and experience as the employee. *Inman v. Fannie Mae*, 2007-SOX-47, at *47 (ALJ March 5, 2008); see also *Livingston v. Wyeth Inc.*, No. 06-1939, 2008 WL 756068 (4th Cir. March 24 2008) (the SOX whistleblower provision requires both a subjectively and an objectively reasonable belief that the employer's conduct constitutes a violation of relevant law).

SOX whistleblower claims are filed with the U.S. Occupational Safety and Health Administration, the agency responsible for the initial investigation. The next level is a hearing before a U.S. Department of Labor administrative law judge. The administrative law judge's decision may be appealed to the U.S. Department of Labor Administrative Review Board, and from there to the U.S. Court of Appeals.

As in Title VII retaliation cases, the SOX claimant bears the burden of demonstrating that the protected activity was a contributing factor in the adverse personnel action. 29 C.F.R. §1980.104. Even a small action, such as calling an ethics hotline or objecting to certain job duties, can trigger protection under SOX. See, e.g., *Hendrix v. American Airlines Inc.*, 2004-SOX-23, at 3 (ALJ December 9, 2004) (employee who provided information to employer during investigation of another employee engaged in a protected activity); *Hughart v. Raymond James & Assocs.*, 2004-SOX-9, at

3 (ALJ December 17, 2004) (employee engaged in protected activity by speaking to supervisor and sending her a "fraud alert" e-mail regarding irregularities in certain trades executed by the employer). The employer can defeat a SOX claim by demonstrating that the protected activity was not a factor in its personnel decision, or that it would have taken the same adverse action in the absence of the protected activity. 49 U.S.C. §42121(b)(2)(B)(iv).

Remedies for Employees Who Bring SOX Whistleblower Claims

SOX provides that a prevailing employee is "entitled to all relief necessary to make the employee whole." 18 U.S.C. §1514A(c). The act further states that compensatory damages shall include reinstatement, back pay, and "compensation for any special damages sustained as a result of the discrimination, including litigation costs, expert witness fees, and reasonable attorney fees." Id. Case law predating SOX generally limits "special damages" to pecuniary damages (i.e., damages capable of being estimated in a dollar amount) that result from a specific event, such as loss of a specific contract or other business opportunity. Non-pecuniary damages, such as emotional distress or injury to reputation, typically have not been included.

In SOX cases, however, there is a split of authority regarding the availability of non-pecuniary damages. For example, a federal court in the Eastern District of New York last year held that an employee might recover damages for harm to his reputation under the SOX whistleblower provision. *Mahony v. KeySpan Corp.*, No. 04 CV 554 SJ, 2007 WL 805813, at *7 (E.D.N.Y. March 12, 2007). In another recent case, an administrative law judge tied monetary and reputational injuries together by awarding $642,941 to a successful SOX plaintiff to compensate for "the diminution in expected earnings in all of her future jobs for as long as the reputational injury is expected to affect her prospects." *Hagman v. Washington Mut. Bank*, 2005-SOX-73, at 40 (ALJ December 19, 2006); compare *Hanna v. WCI Communities Inc.*, 348 F. Supp. 2d 1332, 1334 (S.D. Fla. 2004) (reputational damages are available under SOX based on language that allows a prevailing employee to recover "all relief necessary to make the employee whole"), with *Walton v. Nova Info. Sys.*, 514 F. Supp. 2d 1031, 1035 (E.D. Tenn. 2007) (SOX whistleblower provision does not provide for recovery of non-pecuniary damages such as injury to reputation, mental and physical distress, or punitive damages), and *Murray v. TXU Corp.*, No. CIV.A.3:03-CV-0888-P, 2005 WL 1356444, at **2-3 (N.D. Tex. June 7, 2005) (SOX does not provide for any type of non-pecuniary damages, including reputational damages). Until the split of authority on this important issue is resolved, the stakes are likely to remain high in SOX retaliation cases.

In addition to special damages, another important remedy available in a SOX whistleblower case is reinstatement. Unlike many other anti-retaliation statutes, reinstatement is a presumptive remedy in a SOX whistleblower case. Moreover, an administrative law judge's order to reinstate must be implemented immediately, regardless of whether an appeal is filed. As a practical matter, this means an employee may demand a premium to settle a case without reinstatement of the employee.

Proper Documentation in SOX Cases

Proper documentation is as important in SOX whistleblower cases as it is in other retaliation cases. Documentation is particularly important if an employee who participated in a SOX investigation subsequently faces termination or other discipline based on the results of the investigation. Experienced counsel can advise human resources officials regarding disciplinary decisions. Employers who may wish to argue that a SOX investigation is protected by the attorney/client privilege may find it helpful to document employee discipline measures separate and apart from any report of the investigation of alleged corporate misconduct. Because SOX is still fairly new, employers and the courts are still framing many whistleblower issues. Even in the absence of more comprehensive guidance, however, employers will benefit from putting appropriate policies and procedures in place.

Key Players in Resolving SOX Disputes

SOX retaliation claims by their very nature raise complex legal questions, such as whether Securities and Exchange Commission regulations or federal laws relating to fraud against shareholders have been violated. That means executives who oversee the particular area of SOX compliance at issue (i.e., the subject of the whistleblower complaint) will have an important role to play in resolving a SOX complaint. Legal counsel will also be needed to analyze the facts under applicable law and determine the company's potential exposure. Some companies prefer to use outside attorneys who do not regularly represent the company. Hiring independent counsel may increase the company's credibility with regulators and help ensure that key communications and legal advice provided to the company are protected by the attorney/client privilege or the work product doctrine. While the legal and compliance issues may sometimes overshadow the human resources issues, input from human resources officials is still important.

Extraterritorial Reach of SOX Whistleblower Cases

Several recent cases have grappled with the jurisdictional reach of SOX. One such case raises the possibility of employer liability for retaliation against whistleblowers residing outside the United States. The issue presented was whether a U.S. employee of a foreign company who was working abroad is protected by the SOX whistleblower provision. See *O'Mahony v. Accenture Ltd.*, No. 07 CIV. 7916, 2008 WL 344710 (S.D.N.Y. February 5, 2008). The employee in that case initially worked for a U.S. subsidiary of a foreign company, and then transferred to a position with the company's French subsidiary. Id. at *1. The U.S. subsidiary continued to pay the employee's compensation after the transfer. The employee alleged that while she was working for the French subsidiary, the company refused to pay her French Social Security contributions and concealed the fact that she was working in France. After the employee objected to this treatment, an executive of the U.S. subsidiary purportedly reduced her level of job responsibility. Id.

The employee initially filed a SOX whistleblower complaint with the Occupational Safety and Health Administration, which dismissed her claim, stating that "the [U.S. Department of Labor] lacked jurisdiction over the claim because §1514A [the SOX whistleblower provision] does not apply extraterritorially." 2008 WL 344710, at *2. Because of a procedural quirk, the employee was permitted to seek review in the U.S. District Court for the Southern District of New York. The federal district court held that the employee was entitled to SOX whistleblower protection, distinguishing a previous First Circuit case, which held that the statute did not apply extraterritorially. See *Carnero v. Boston Scientific Corp.*, 433 F.3d 1 (1st Cir.) (SOX whistleblower provision did not protect an employee who was a foreign citizen employed by a foreign subsidiary of an American company), cert. denied, 126 S. Ct. 2973 (2006).

Applying a "conduct" test, the *O'Mahony* court found that "the commission of the alleged fraud and the decision by [the U.S. subsidiary] to retaliate against O'Mahony, occurred primarily in the United States." 2008 WL 344710, at *7. The court reasoned that the employee was paid by the U.S. subsidiary during the alleged fraud, the conduct related to the alleged fraud involved employees of the company who were located in the United States, the misconduct itself occurred in the United States, and the alleged retaliatory actions were taken by executives located in the United States and employed by the U.S. subsidiary. Id. at *7-8. Under these circumstances, the court held that extending whistleblower protection to an overseas employee of a foreign affiliate of a SOX company was appropriate. Id. at *9.

Defining "Protected Activity"

Determining whether a claimant engaged in "protected activity" is a critical issue in a SOX whistleblower case. According to the statute, protected activity occurs when an employee engages in any lawful act "to provide information, cause information to be provided, or otherwise assist in an investigation regarding any conduct which the employee reasonably believes constitutes a violation" of the federal laws and regulations listed in the whistleblower provision. See 18 U.S.C. §1514A(a)(1). Several recent cases have helped to understand what this means in practice.

The issue in the first case was whether assisting a co-worker who raised concerns with management regarding improper accounting methods is protected activity under SOX. See *Mahony v. KeySpan Corp.*, No. 04 CV 554 SJ, 2007 WL 805813 (E.D.N.Y. March 12, 2007). The court held that assisting a co-worker who reports potential fraud is protected, stating that SOX applies to "those who make the whistle audible" as well as "those who blow the whistle." Id. at *5. The court found that the employee in *Mahony* was engaged in protected activity even though he was only "opening a channel of communication" between the whistleblower and the company's chief executive officer by encouraging the chief executive officer to attend a meeting with the whistleblower. Id. The court reasoned, "Given that SOX is a statute designed to promote corporate ethics by protecting whistleblowers from retaliation, it is reasonable to construe the statute broadly." Id.

In another case that defines the scope of protected activity under SOX, the Administrative Review Board confirmed that an employee must reasonably believe the company is engaged in one of the types of violations protected by SOX to establish a claim under the whistleblower provision. In *Welch v. Cardinal Bankshares Corp.*, ARB No. 05-064, ALJ No. 2003-SOX-15 (ARB May 31, 2007), the Administrative Review Board held that an employee did not engage in protected activity because he could not reasonably have believed a report filed with the Securities and Exchange Commission presented a misleading picture of the company's financial condition. 2003-SOX-15, at 11. Additionally, the board held that allegations that the company rejected the chief financial officer's accounting advice and allowed employees with no accounting expertise to access the company's general ledger could not be reasonably regarded as violations of the federal securities laws. Id. at 13-14. Importantly, the decision notes that only reports of violations of the federal laws and regulations listed in the SOX whistleblower provision trigger protection under the statute. Id. at 13. The chief financial officer's complaint that he lacked access to company auditors was not related to federal securities laws, and therefore was not protected by the SOX whistleblower provision. Id. This development is significant for companies, because it strengthens a potential defense that complaints regarding violations that fall outside the federal laws and regulations listed in the statute are not protected by SOX.

Another recent case confirms that to establish a SOX whistleblower claim, an employee must have an objectively reasonable belief that the employer violated one of the federal laws listed in the whistleblower statute. In *Allen v. Administrative Review Board*, 514 F.3d 468, 471-74 (5th Cir. 2008), several employees raised concerns as to whether the company's computer and accounting systems complied with Securities and Exchange Commission guidelines. The employees alleged that because of raising their concerns, they began to experience hostile treatment and were eventually terminated in a workforce reduction. Id. at 473-75. An administrative law judge dismissed their claim, and the Administrative Review Board affirmed the judge's decision. Id. at 471.

The U.S. Court of Appeals for the Fifth Circuit reviewed the Administrative Review Board's decision and agreed that the employees had not engaged in protected activity. Id. at 476. The court first addressed allegations regarding the employer's internal financial documents that the employee, a certified public accountant, knew were not subject to Securities and Exchange Commission guidelines. Id. at 478-79. The court held that given the employee's expertise in accounting, she could not have reasonably believed her employer was violating a "rule or regulation of the [Securities and Exchange Commission]" through internal financial documents, and therefore raising concerns over this issue was not activity protected by SOX. Id. The court then turned to allegations that the employer failed to disclose to its shareholders that problems with its computer and accounting systems could negatively affect the company's financial condition. Id. at 481-82. The court held that these allegations were not the type of concerns for shareholder fraud protected by SOX, because an employee must reasonably believe the company acted with an intent to "deceive, manipulate, or defraud" its shareholders, rather than merely acted negligently. Id. at 479-80. The court affirmed the Administrative Review Board's ruling and agreed that the employee failed to establish this essential element during the hearing. Id. at 480-82; see also *Adam v. Fannie Mae*, 2007-SOX-50, at 4-5 (ALJ February 25, 2008) (granting summary decision for employer where employee alleged that he reported to his employer that certain vendors were committing fraud against the company but failed to show that the company knew of the fraud or otherwise intended to deceive its shareholders).

Companies should expect to see more decisions that define the scope of protected activity under the SOX whistleblower provision.

Adapting Defense Strategies to SOX Whistleblower Claims

As SOX whistleblower claims continue to increase, companies and attorneys are developing creative strategies to defend against these claims depending upon the specific needs of each employer. Litigation strategies to minimize exposure include legal principles available to employers in traditional employment disputes. For example, depending upon the circumstances of each case, it may be possible to use offers of judgment or apply the after-acquired evidence doctrine to minimize liability in a SOX case.

In typical employment disputes, the Federal Rules of Civil Procedure allow employers to offer to have judgment entered against them on specified terms. See Fed. R. Civ. P. 68. If the offer is accepted, the lawsuit is over. If the offer is rejected and the employee eventually obtains a judgment that is "not more favorable" than the offer, the employee must pay any defense costs incurred after the offer was made. An offer of judgment may reduce costs for companies by increasing settlement pressure and allowing employers to recover litigation costs. While the SOX whistleblower provision provides equitable remedies such as reinstatement that may not be easily reduced to a monetary amount, an offer of judgment can be a useful tool to foster settlement when back pay is a primary concern.

The after-acquired evidence doctrine may provide another means of limiting an employer's damages in the SOX context. When an employer has terminated an employee for an allegedly illegal reason and subsequently discovers evidence that would have resulted in termination for a clearly legitimate reason, reinstatement and front pay are inappropriate remedies, and the employee is limited to back pay from the date of termination to the date of discovery of the new information. Thus, the after-acquired evidence doctrine can be a useful tool to defend against reinstatement, the presumptive remedy under SOX. See *Welch v. Cardinal Bankshares Corp.*, 2003-SOX-15, at **2-5 (ALJ February 15, 2005) (analyzing the after-acquired evidence doctrine in the context of a SOX whistleblower claim).

Obtaining a Valid Release of a SOX Claim

When an employer offers a severance payment in exchange for the employee's signed release, the employer generally intends that release to cover all possible claims. In the employment context, however, this may not always be possible, particularly under certain remedial statutes such as the Family Medical Leave Act and the Fair Labor Standards Act. For instance, an employee may not waive his or her rights to minimum wages and overtime under the Fair Labor Standards Act in consideration for payment of less than the statutorily prescribed amount. 29 U.S.C. §253(a); *D.A. Schulte, Inc. v. Gangi*, 328 U.S. 108, 114-16 (1946). Similarly, an apparent ambiguity in the Family Medical Leave Act regulatory language has led to a split of authority among certain courts as to whether employees may waive any of their rights under the act. See 29 C.F.R. §825.220; *Taylor v. Progress*

Energy Inc., 493 F.3d 454, 459 (4th Cir. 2007) (interpreting Family Medical Leave Act regulations to prohibit prospective and retroactive waiver of any such rights, including the right to file a claim for damages), petition for cert. filed, 76 U.S.L.W. 3226 (U.S. October 22, 2007) (No. 07-539); *Faris v. Williams WPC-I Inc.*, 332 F.3d 316, 322 (5th Cir. 2003) (an employee cannot execute a prospective release of substantive rights (such as leave and reinstatement) under the Family Medical Leave Act, but may execute a retroactive waiver of damages claims).

A concurring opinion in a recent Administrative Review Board decision provides support for the position that a release of "all claims" in an employee severance agreement encompasses SOX whistleblower claims. *Moldauer v. Canandaigua Wine Co.*, ARB No. 04-022, 2005 WL 4891658, at *13-14 (December 30, 2005).

In *Canandaigua Wine*, the employee, Edwin Moldauer, entered into a severance agreement with his former employer, Canandaigua Wine Company, which contained broad language releasing Canandaigua from "all claims" related to Moldauer's employment or termination. Id. at *6, 13. Moldauer filed a SOX whistleblower complaint. Canandaigua moved to dismiss Moldauer's complaint on the grounds that he had released his SOX whistleblower claim in the severance agreement, and that his complaint was untimely. The administrative law judge dismissed the case, and Moldauer appealed, arguing that he was entitled to equitable tolling of the statute of limitations and equitable modification of the severance agreement on the ground that Canandaigua failed to disclose the existence of SOX during negotiations.

The Administrative Review Board dismissed Moldauer's complaint based upon his failure to timely file. Judge Beyer, one of the three administrative law judges who comprised the Administrative Review Board, concurred with the decision, but wrote separately to address what he viewed as the threshold issue: whether Moldauer's claims were validly released in the severance agreement. Id. at *5. In examining this issue, Judge Beyer relied upon employment discrimination cases involving employee releases of claims under the Americans with Disabilities Act, the Age Discrimination in Employment Act, and Title VII, treating such claims as analogous to SOX whistleblower claims. Id. at *10-12. He concluded that, as in the related contexts of the Americans with Disabilities Act, the Age Discrimination in Employment Act, and Title VII, Moldauer had validly released his SOX whistleblower claims pursuant to the broad "all claims" language contained in the agreement. Id. at *13.

Although Judge Beyer's concurrence may not be binding on administrative law judges who hear SOX cases, it can be cited for its persuasive value. By likening the waiver of SOX whistleblower claims to those under the Americans with Disabilities Act, the Age Discrimination in Employment Act, and Title VII, Judge Beyer lent credence to the view that employers should be able to purchase a release of these claims as well. The *Canandaigua Wine* concurrence should also provide guidance to federal judges who may address this issue as a matter of first impression. Nonetheless, including a specific reference to SOX whistleblower claims may avoid the need to litigate the scope of the release.

Key Company Procedures and Policies in a SOX Dispute

While many employers have anti-retaliation policies, many of those policies do not refer to SOX. An anti-retaliation policy or employee hotline that specifically refers to SOX may provide a stronger defense against whistleblower claims than one that does not. As employees file more and more SOX whistleblower claims, employers are finding it useful to implement reporting and investigation procedures of the kind used to address employee complaints of retaliation and age, race, or gender discrimination. Depending upon each employer's particular circumstances, these procedures could include:

- A written policy prohibiting discrimination or retaliation against whistleblowers and delineating the procedures for employees to follow if they believe they have been subjected to discrimination or retaliation. A written policy increases awareness and protects employers by guiding management decisions that may implicate the SOX whistleblower provision. If a claim is filed, a well-written policy serves as a strong defense and may provide leverage to resolve the claim early before incurring significant litigation costs.
- A specified procedure for reporting alleged corporate misconduct. Requiring employees to follow a specific set of written procedures

for reporting corporate misconduct will make the complaint procedure more understandable for employees and make corporations aware of the alleged violation.

- A specified procedure for determining when an allegation of corporate misconduct should be referred to the audit committee of the board of directors, and when to involve outside counsel.
- A commitment to investigate all complaints of corporate misconduct and to apprise the complaining employee of any resolution.
- A commitment to take appropriate action with respect to any retaliation against a complaining employee.

Companies must respond quickly and effectively to concerns raised by employees who may have whistleblower protection. During the next several years, we expect more employers to adopt internal reporting procedures for SOX concerns so they may respond immediately when a complaint is received.

Final Thoughts

SOX whistleblower claims present a unique intersection of employment law, securities law, corporate governance, and in some cases, government investigation. Because SOX investigations by their very nature involve legal questions, such as whether Securities and Exchange Commission regulations or federal laws relating to fraud against shareholders have been violated, companies will generally find it desirable to retain competent outside counsel with experience in all areas implicated by SOX. Companies often find that a full-service law firm with strong experience in litigation and securities law is best suited to investigate and respond to complaints under the SOX whistleblower provision.

Allegra Lawrence-Hardy is a partner with Sutherland Asbill & Brennan LLP. She is co-chair of the firm's complex business litigation group. Her practice includes commercial litigation and labor and employment law. She has represented companies throughout the United States and abroad in numerous trials and other forums. She has litigated cases in federal and state courts for primarily Fortune 100 companies from California to New York, and she has extensive experience negotiating complex settlements and finding creative solutions. She is regularly quoted in the media as a leading practitioner in her field.

Ms. Lawrence-Hardy has been ranked by Chambers USA, *and* Georgia Trend *magazine recognized her as one of "Forty Under Forty" rising stars in Georgia in 2003. The magazine has repeatedly named her in the "Legal Elite." The* Fulton County Daily Report *featured her in its annual "On the Rise" issue, and* Atlanta Woman *named her one of "Atlanta's Twenty-Five Power Women to Watch."* Atlanta *magazine also has repeatedly named her a "Georgia Super Lawyer," as well as regularly recognized her in its "Top Fifty Female Georgia Super Lawyers."*

Ms. Lawrence-Hardy earned her B.A., magna cum laude, from Spelman College and her J.D. from Yale Law School. She is a member of numerous professional organizations and boards of directors, and she is an avid writer in her areas of expertise.

Basic Thoughts on Representing Companies in Employment Matters

Samuel M. Matchett

Partner

King & Spalding

ASPATORE

Introduction

After law school, I was a judicial clerk before moving to an in-house position with the country's largest department store chain. As an in-house lawyer, I dealt with a number of different areas, including employment law, which I found to be the most dynamic and interesting. After four years, I went into private practice and focused on employment law exclusively. By specializing in employment law, I honed in on what I enjoyed most about the practice of law, which is dealing with the human dynamic and the often simple, often complex, relationships between employers and employees.

I often think of employment law as industrial domestic relations (a phrase borrowed from my friend and mentor). Outside of one's relationship with family, the defining relationship in a person's life is usually their job. When you are hired, promoted, get bonuses, or receive some positive recognition in the workplace, those are all aspects of a good employment situation, and when things go well on the job, people are extremely happy. However, when things go badly in the workplace, employees experience the opposite end of the emotional scale. Indeed, emotion has a lot to do with the practice of employment law, much as it does in domestic relationships, which adds to the dynamic of this practice area and makes it so interesting.

Key Focus in Employment Law

The types of cases I handle on a frequent basis include race discrimination claims, age claims, gender claims, and Family Medical Leave Act claims. Additionally, we are seeing a great rise in retaliation claims, largely because the Supreme Court's pronouncements in this area have made it easier to maintain those types of claims. Basically, an action by the employer that can reasonably be viewed as discharging or punishing an employee for asserting his or her right to protect alleged discrimination may constitute retaliation. I also represent federal contractors or subcontractors that are subject to the affirmative action-related Executive Order 11246, and are being audited by the Office of Federal Contract Compliance Programs. There has also been a rise in cases involving restrictive covenants—clients who are looking to enforce covenants not to compete or solicit employees, as well as clients who need to know whether a restrictive covenant that a newly hired employee entered into with a previous employer is enforceable. Many times, we wind up defending temporary restraining order litigation with respect to restrictive covenants, or pursuing that line of offense on behalf of our clients. Finally, wage and hour claims have risen substantially, and we have been dealing with many collective actions in that area.

Counseling and preventative training is also a substantial part of my practice, and I assist many clients with their employment issues as a preventative measure. In many cases, we assess what the client has been experiencing, and we evaluate whether there has been a rise in particular types of employment claims. We spend significant time training the client's employee population, particularly those at the supervisor and management level, a process that involves reinforcing existing policies and practices, and developing strategies to address issues that may give rise to employment disputes. Anti-discrimination and harassment training, for example, educate employees on their rights and responsibilities, on the employers' policies, and provides an opportunity to ask and have their questions answered.

A Unique Approach to Labor Law

I believe that having started my career as an in-house lawyer who closely partnered with clients in the business world, rather than as a private practice lawyer, has worked to my advantage in this practice area. When you work in a law firm as a new lawyer, you often work on small pieces of a case (e.g., a research project, interviewing a witness), and you are not the one who is in charge of the entire matter. However, as an in-house lawyer, I started out by viewing the big picture and working backwards. I needed to understand what the company's goals were, the impact of a particular decision on the company and on the individuals involved. This information informed my approach to the case. Today, I continue to apply that in-house lawyer mindset to my employment law practice. One of the first things I consider when taking on a new client case is whether I fully understand the client's business and their goals (i.e., how their business functions, who the key players are, what this piece of litigation means for the specific department that is impacted, what it means for the company, and how the company can be positioned to its advantage), and not solely from the standpoint of defending this specific lawsuit.

Most importantly, I need to make sure I have sufficient information to (1) understand how the issue arose, (2) address the factors that led to the issue arising, and (3) determine whether there are any internal or systemic issues, or factors that need to be addressed. For example, I need to know what the current dispute means in terms of the overall morale of those employees who are still working for the company and who may be familiar—or think they are familiar—with the facts of this situation, and I want to understand how the claim impacts the client's ability to continue with its business. There are many lawyers who can provide very good advice, but it is important for that legal advice to be married to the client's business goals and realities. As an in-house lawyer, I always focused on understanding what the company's business goals were, because that knowledge could inform what will ultimately constitute a win-win situation for both parties in an employment dispute. For example, it does not make good business sense to spend $300,000 to win a case of age discrimination against an employee who makes only $30,000 a year. In such a case, it is important to determine whether there is some other route we can take to reach a settlement (e.g., internal or external dispute resolution/mediation, or a resolution at the Equal Employment Opportunity Commission level, or perhaps we can find a job opportunity that the person who is bringing the claim would be appropriate for). Defending a claim in litigation is just one of the options to consider in an employment dispute, based on understanding the company's goals and needs.

Preliminary Client Meetings: Representing an Ongoing Client

When taking on an employment dispute case for an ongoing client—someone I have been representing for some time—my initial approach is to partner with someone in human resources or on the business side with whom I have an existing relationship so I can find out what the dispute is all about. For example, if there has been a claim of gender discrimination or harassment against a manager in a certain department, I will say to my internal confidante, "You know the people and the personalities in that department. What can you tell me about its history? How long has the manager been with the company? Have any prior claims, incidents, or rumors come out of that department?" I find that this type of interview helps me in two ways. First, it helps give me a the proverbial "lay of the land," and second, by making references to company history, people, and buzz words, I can convey to my contact that I really know their company, and I know what is going on there. I want them to think of me as someone who is not a hired gun, but as someone who is trying to understand what really happened in relation to the employment dispute. Hopefully, this approach will give my confidante a greater comfort level in terms of talking to me—and it will make them aware that they cannot mislead me with respect to what is going on in the company.

I also obtain some background and quasi-statistical information in relation to the claim. For example, I might research all of the promotions that occurred in the department in question over the last few years. I also find it useful to look at some of the case law that is attendant to the particular claim, and I use two key desk resources—*Linderman & Grossman*, which is the employment handbook bible and a great resource for refreshing your knowledge in a particular area; and *Garland Employment Law Updates*. Over the years, I have developed a practice of jotting down recent cases I think are interesting, novel, or otherwise important, in a notebook I have divided into various subject matter categories. I often consult that notebook when I am dictating a motion for summary judgment, or when I am looking at the facts of a particular case, and I want to have a sense of the latest law in that area or obtain an understanding of some hard-to-find legal concept. Consequently, if I am handling an age discrimination claim, I will pull out my notebook and look over some of the more recent cases I have put in there.

If the client is facing a lawsuit, I will also research the attorney for the other party, as well as the judge and magistrate judge who are involved. I will send an e-mail to my colleagues to find out if they know the lawyer on the other side, or if they have had experiences with a certain judge.

Representing a New Client in an Employment Dispute

When I am dealing with a client I have not worked with before—a client who may have come to me as the result of a referral from another client, an employment law seminar where I was a presenter, or a direct pitch—I will typically do some of the same things I do for an ongoing client, but there is a little more work involved, because I do not have the deep and abiding relationships I have with an ongoing client. In such cases, my associates and

I will work, generally without charge, to learn all we can about the client's business. For example, if we have a client who handles outsourcing jobs for airlines and airports, I will read their materials, visit their Web site, and spend time on the ground learning what the client's people do. In most cases, we will meet with the client's human resources manager or a businessperson and follow them around to see what they do on a first-hand basis. We also try to identify some of the key people we hope to work with in human resources and on the business side, and we meet with them to get to know them and talk about their respective jobs and daily concerns.

Essentially, we are trying to get to know the client's business and key players so we can best represent them—and it is difficult to understand a client's business and business goals if I only sit in my office. It is always important to put in some face time—to make an investment in terms of getting to know the client without charging them for that research process.

When working with a new client, we will always ask them what has been happening at the company in terms of previous employment disputes, and if there have been a number of state and federal administrative charges, we will suggest training programs that would be helpful to the company going forward. Our hope is that the client will establish and maintain a long relationship with us. Therefore, we want to offer preventative assistance with respect to possible future issues, while assisting the client with the issue that has already occurred.

Obtaining Key Documentation and Evidence

There are three specific ways plaintiffs can go about proving their case in an employment dispute: by presenting direct evidence, circumstantial evidence, or statistical evidence. Therefore, at the outset of my representation, I will pose questions to the client that relate to the different methods of proof a plaintiff has available to prove their case.

Direct evidence is an oral or written statement that evinces discriminatory intent. For example, let us say the plaintiff in a gender discrimination case is charging that a manager in her company told a co-worker that even though she was the most qualified employee for a position, he would not hire a woman to work in his department, or the manager sent that same message to someone in an e-mail. It is illegal under Title VII of the Civil Rights Act of 1964 to discriminate on the basis of gender or sex. Therefore, any such written or oral statements made by a hiring manager constitute direct evidence that they considered the plaintiff's gender when they were making an adverse employment decision. Consequently, it is always important to ask your client if they have any knowledge of written or oral statements that might evince discrimination. You must also tell your client to put a hold on any e-mails or documents that relate to the plaintiff's employment, or that mention the plaintiff's name.

Statistical evidence is not typically used in an individual claim of discrimination. It is often used when there is a claim of adverse impact. But even in an individual case, statistics can be used to raise a presumption or inference of discrimination. If the plaintiff says she was not promoted into a department because she is a woman, I will ask the client to give me the statistical information on that department for the past few years, including the gender breakdown in the department at the present time, how many women have been promoted into that department in the recent past, and who has been considered for openings in that department. Looking at such statistics can help give us a sense for whether the numbers would indicate that something is amiss.

Finally, discrimination can be proved through circumstantial evidence, and the courts have come up with a proof paradigm, with the first requiring that a plaintiff is required to establish an inference of discrimination. Therefore, I will ask my client for documents that indicate whether the individual suffered an adverse employment action or was treated less favorably than someone similarly situated who is not in the same protected class. If the employer is able to provide a legitimate, non-discriminatory reason for the plaintiff's treatment, the plaintiff might have to establish pretext (that the employer's stated reason for the employment action is a lie). Determining whether the plaintiff is in a protected category (race, ethnicity, gender, sex, age, religion, disability, etc.) is usually easy to substantiate. You also need to investigate whether the plaintiff was qualified for the job, and what their on-the-job conduct was like.

If the individual was subjected to an adverse employment action such as being passed over for a promotion, you want to obtain any documentation related to that event (i.e., who was considered for the job and what their background was, and who ultimately got the job, including whether that individual was outside the same protected category as the individual making the claim). Therefore, you will need to obtain the personnel file and any other documentation the client might have with respect to the individual who actually got the job, as well as others who were considered, to show why the selected individual was more qualified for the job than the plaintiff.

I will also ask the employer for information relating to the company's promotion process. If the company has a specific promotion policy, or job posting policy for an open position, I need to know whether those policies were followed in relation to the particular event that is in dispute, and I will want to see any written policies as well as any information or documents relating to general practices in that area.

I will also ask the client about any key witnesses. For example, in the hypothetical when the manager was overheard to say the plaintiff was qualified for the position, but he did not want to bring a woman into an all-male employee department, I will need to know the background of the individual who reported that remark in order to make sure they have not made similar claims to human resources that have never been substantiated. It may turn out that the witness has a problem with telling the truth, or is an attention seeker.

Handling Disputes Internally: The Open Door Process

An employment-related dispute often comes to light through a company's open door process, which may involve bringing a complaint to a manager. The company then has an opportunity to deal with the issue internally before any external parties are involved. In other situations, the company may not learn of an issue until an administrative charge has been filed with a state or federal agency, and those entities will routinely invite the parties to discuss case resolution or mediation at the outset of the investigation. In other cases, a lawsuit will be filed by the plaintiff, and the parties may then decide to informally discuss and resolve the case with or without the use of a mediator. Or pursuant to court directive, the parties might be required to engage in a non-binding mediation process.

If the plaintiff has used the company's internal open door process—which may entail going to human resources or their manager to articulate their problem—that is the best time to try to resolve the issue. If a dispute is handled internally, the company can save outside attorneys' fees, and the emotional aspects of the matter will not get ratcheted up. At this time, it is important to establish the facts of the dispute. An in-house lawyer's job is not to assume the company is right in all instances. It is to learn the facts and properly advise their client based on the law and the company's goals. If an employee has come forward and complained about something, it is important to thank the person for raising the issue, even if you do not agree with their viewpoint, because that individual has acted pursuant to the company's stated goal of resolving matters internally, and has made use of its open door policy. It is important to listen to the employee and talk to those people who have the facts and information.

Next, the company needs to determine whether there is any merit to the individual's claim, keeping in mind that the perception of wrongdoing is not the same as actual wrongdoing. Many laypeople think perceived mistreatment equals illegality, and that is simply not the case. Discrimination is not illegal—illegal discrimination is illegal. We make discriminating decisions every day of our lives. For example, if the company has one open position and it has five excellent candidates, management will need to make a discriminating decision and select the candidate they think is best. Therefore, discrimination is only illegal if there is a specific statute or legal precept that makes it illegal.

However, you must also look at the merits of what the employee is claiming, irrespective of the legal validity of the claim, because it does not benefit the company to have an employee who has a perception that he or she is being mistreated, or that the policies, procedures, and benefits of the company do not apply equally to him or her. If you do not believe the employee is being unreasonable, you should try to address the situation in a way that is mutually agreeable so you can nip in the bud what could evolve into a much more inflammatory situation. For example, an employee who has a personality conflict with a co-worker or supervisor may not have a legal claim, but addressing the conflict will resolve a workplace issue that could evolve into a meritless claim of discrimination.

Sometimes an internal resolution can be reached by simply explaining a hiring or promotion process to the employee. In other cases, you need to get the two parties together in the same room so they can communicate as adults and talk face to face to achieve some form of resolution. In some cases, the employee's complaint is simply unfounded, and while you may not be able to resolve matters to the employee's satisfaction, just going through the process is often sufficient to head off any further issues.

In other situations, you may need to go outside of the department where the conflict exists, and involve an internal person who can make decisions over and above what a particular manager in that particular group might make. For example, some companies have, in conjunction with their open door process, an internal grievance procedure. For example, employees should go to their manager with a complaint unless the manager is involved in the problem, in which case they would go to another specified individual. If that does not work, they would go to a person in human resources who will serve as a neutral decision-maker; if that does not work there may be a group of individuals who work outside of the employee's department who will listen to the grievance and make a decision about what is appropriate, or make a recommendation to an appropriate decision-maker regarding the situation.

Administrative Agency Charges

If an employee has filed an administrative charge against the employer (e.g., an Equal Employment Opportunity Commission charge or a charge filed with an agency such as the California Fair Employment and Housing Office), the employer will receive notice of the charge, a request for a position statement, and in many cases a request for mediation. Whether the employer will decide to mediate will be determined by an understanding of the facts of the case, as well as an understanding of the law as applied to those facts. In many cases when a grievance is filed, internally the law is less important, because if the person is complaining through an open door process they are still employed, and in those cases, you do not want to have a disgruntled employee who is poisoning the environment. You want to address that person's concern regardless of whether the issue they are raising has legal validity. However, once an employee has filed a claim externally, understanding the potential legal merit of the claim in addition to the facts of the matter is very important, because you are essentially trying to determine whether their claim could turn into something larger that could cost you a lot of time and money.

When deciding whether to mediate or resolve the matter early on, you will need to evaluate how much time and expense will be involved in having your human resources and businesspeople track down the facts of the claim, and what your typical experience has been with this particular Equal Employment Opportunity Commission office or investigator. Do they tend to be neutral or hostile to employers, and is the mediator someone who can help both sides see the strengths and weaknesses of their case? You must also consider whether the employee is still working at your company and how much they make. If the employee does not make a lot of money, settling for a small amount might be a good idea, even though there does not appear to be any legal merit to the case. Also, you need to consider who the witnesses in the case will be. You may have a great case, but horrible witnesses—people who are not good in adversarial situations. In other instances, you may not have all of the needed documentation in place, but you may have strong witnesses.

The decision about whether to mediate or engage in dispute resolution on the administrative level will come down to whether you have a strong legal position and an economic analysis. If you have a strong position, but the employee is no longer with your company, and it will cost you a considerable amount of money to have your outside counsel prepare a position statement, it may make better economic sense to settle the matter quickly. On the other hand, if the person is still employed, that economic analysis is very different. Employers are typically much more willing to pay to defend an administrative claim that has been filed by someone who is still employed by the company, because if you choose to settle there is a good chance you are simply buying yourself an employee who is going to have an attitude issue, or feels they have put the company in a position where it will be fearful of confronting the employee again (the "invincible employee" syndrome). If the individual has a strong legal claim, we will also factor in what we think the Equal Employment Opportunity Commission will be prepared to do as the charge progresses. Will they want to come on-site and interview other individuals in an effort to convert this claim from an individual charge to a collective claim? If that is the case, I would advise the employer to take appropriate steps to decrease the likelihood of the on-site meeting.

Employment Litigation

If an employment lawsuit has already been filed, it is important to consider all of the previously mentioned factors, with the addition of attorneys' fees. We have a legal system that allows an individual to file a claim of discrimination against a company not with impunity, but quite close to it. An employee can file an Equal Employment Opportunity Commission charge for free—the investigation is done by the administrative agency. A plaintiff can file a lawsuit on a contingency fee basis, putting little, if any, money into the lawsuit. And if a plaintiff loses, they are not liable for the defendant's attorneys' fees. On the other hand, the company that is being charged or sued has to hire attorneys and pay them, and if the plaintiff wins, the defendant almost always has to pay the plaintiff's attorneys' fees. The idea behind this system is that a company is in a better position to pay legal fees than an individual, and an individual might be less likely to pursue the vindication of their legal rights if they knew they may have to pay the defendant's attorneys' fees if they lose. One can debate the pros and cons of the system, and whether there should be some sliding scale payment of fees, but the current system puts a plaintiff in a position where they can file a lawsuit without having to worry about having to write their employer a big check at the end.

Thus, attorneys' fees often become a huge incentive for employers to mediate or seek other forms of alternative dispute resolution. As a lawsuit moves forward and attorneys' fees add up, it becomes increasingly difficult to resolve the case, because simply too much money has already been invested. In the end, the dollars that may have been spent on settlement have been spent on the lawsuit—not only on attorneys' fees, but also on any expert fees that might be part of the litigation. Once a trial commences, everything gets amplified—the emotional level gets ratcheted up, there is increased disruption to the business, attorneys' fees rise, the number of witnesses often multiplies, human resources has to spend more time on the case, and the number of documents you have to put on hold increases. Consequently, many companies choose to pursue case resolution early on through internal alternative dispute resolution mechanisms. In anticipation of such situations, employers will often have employees sign mandatory or non-mandatory arbitration agreements at the outset of their employment. Such companies go beyond the first step of the open door process to create an internal administrative process for resolving disputes. However, while those types of programs replace the litigation process, they do not technically replace the potential remedies one could get through the litigation process—they just change the forum (the employee may no longer have access to a jury trial). Companies that have an internal administrative dispute resolution process will typically implement that process in a series of steps (e.g., open door process, internal mediation, and mandatory arbitration). Ultimately, instead of a lawsuit that could go on three years or more, you have a process that lasts about six months from beginning to end.

Recent Trends in Employment Dispute Resolution

One recent trend in this practice area concerns the increasing number of employers who are reluctant to engage in mandatory arbitration. Both sides have to agree to the arbitrator, who listens to the facts of the case and makes a decision. There is concern on the part of some employers, however, that there is often a tendency for the arbitrator to "split the baby" by ruling in a manner to award and/or punish both sides of the dispute when they are issuing their decision. Consequently, many employers believe they have a better chance of receiving summary judgment in court than in arbitration, and therefore they are increasingly looking for ways to beef up their internal resolution processes short of requiring mandatory arbitration.

Another trend is the rise in restrictive covenants litigation. Companies are very concerned about protecting their trade secrets and proprietary information, and they are very concerned about losing such sensitive information to employees they hire, train, and expose their client lists, strategies, plans, and secret information to. In some cases, an employee may take the information he or she has learned, and the relationships they have gained because of working for a particular company, and make use of them at a new employer. Employees are much more mobile in this decade than in previous decades. Consequently, as employers take steps to protect their trade secret and proprietary information, employees are often asked to sign covenants not to compete or solicit customers or employees. Similarly, a company that hires an employee who is subject to a restrictive covenant with a former employer will often consult us to determine whether the covenant is valid or enforceable before they start investing in training their new employee. Restrictive covenants are not favored in most jurisdictions, but they will generally be upheld if they are reasonable in geographic and temporal scope and the employee is placed on clear notice of what they are prohibited from doing.

Finally, there has been a significant up-tick in wage and hour cases. As previously noted, there are three ways to prove a standard discrimination claim, and the burden of proof remains with the employee. However, a wage and hour case is different. The Fair Labor Standards Act requires that an employer properly classify its employees as exempt or non-exempt from the overtime regulations of the Fair Labor Standards Act. A non-exempt employee who works more than forty hours a week is entitled to time and a half. Wage and hour lawsuits are brought in two categories: classification and unpaid compensation. In classification cases, the employer classified the employee as exempt and did not pay overtime, but the employee alleges they were misclassified. Therefore, the employee seeks back pay for overtime. If a classification mistake holds true for a group of similarly situated employees at the company, the case is brought as a collective action (similar to a class action), and damages can add up to millions of dollars. Significantly, unlike other types of employment litigation, the burden is on the employer to prove it has properly classified its employees and has maintained a record of the employee's working hours. Unfortunately, if the company misclassifies someone as exempt, it probably is not maintaining records of that person's working hours. In unpaid compensation cases, the employee does not dispute their classification but claims they have not been compensated correctly for the hours actually worked. Again, it is the employer's obligation to accurately maintain a record of an employee's hours and to compensate the employee for the work time the employer permits the employee to work.

Samuel M. Matchett is a partner on King & Spalding's Atlanta Labor & Employment Practice Group. He concentrates his practice on employment relationship matters, with an emphasis in labor and employment law litigation in both state and federal courts, governmental agencies, and arbitration tribunals. Mr. Matchett routinely defends employers in litigation involving the Civil Rights Acts of 1866 and 1964 (Title VII), the Age Discrimination in Employment Act, the Americans with Disabilities Act, and employment-related state law claims. Mr. Matchett's practice entails extensive experience in employment discrimination. In addition to his litigation practice, Mr.

Matchett provides general client advice on the avoidance of employee-related problems and presents seminars concerning all aspects of employment law. He is admitted to practice before the United States Supreme Court and several appellate courts.

Mr. Matchett is listed as a leading Labor and Employment lawyer in The Best Lawyers in America, *2007 edition. Additionally, Mr. Matchett was recently selected by* Chambers USA *as a leading lawyer in his practice area and named to* Georgia Trend *magazine's "Legal Elite"—a list of Georgia attorneys chosen by their peers as the leading lawyers in their practice areas. Mr. Matchett is approved by National Union (AIG) for the handling of individual and class action employment and ERISA cases.*

Mr. Matchett co-authored [Juries], [*in*] Employment Litigation Handbook *184 (Jon W. Greene and John W. Robinson IV eds., 1998).*

Mr. Matchett graduated from Morehouse College with a B.A. in 1981. He received his J.D. from the University of Georgia in 1984. Mr. Matchett has served as a faculty member for the Institute of Applied Management and Law (IAML), National Business Institute and Federal Publications. He formally served as a member of the Board of Trustees for the University of Georgia Foundation and is a member of the Board of Governors for the State Bar of Georgia.

Resolving Employment Disputes: Notes from the Field

Douglas T. Schwarz

Partner

Bingham McCutchen LLP

ASPATORE

Introduction

As the number and type of employment laws and employment disputes have grown exponentially in the last two decades, so have professionals' tools and skills in resolving those disputes. This chapter describes one lawyer's reflections on what works and what doesn't, without attempting to be comprehensive, but with an effort to provide some helpful insight.

Early in my legal career, I worked on civil rights and discrimination cases in the civil rights divisions of the U.S. Department of Justice (during law school) and the Massachusetts Office of the Attorney General (after a federal court clerkship). In private practice, I initially did a fair amount of work representing plaintiffs in employment disputes and then shifted my focus to representing companies in claims by their employees. I later served as a commissioner of the Massachusetts Commission against Discrimination. This is the Massachusetts state agency where employees are required to bring claims they have under the Massachusetts Fair Employment Practices Act prior to bringing such claims in court. It is similar to the Equal Employment Opportunity Commission, which handles claims under federal employment discrimination laws. Employees who believe they have been aggrieved by their employer may file their case with the Equal Employment Opportunity Commission, the appropriate state agency, or both. As commissioner of the Massachusetts Commission against Discrimination, I played a number of different roles—sometimes the judge, sometimes the neutral mediator, and sometimes the prosecutor. Spending three years working on every conceivable type of discrimination, harassment, and retaliation claim gave me a broad range of experience with these issues.

My practice today involves representing companies and not-for-profit institutions in all types of employment disputes, including trying cases and arguing appeals, and counseling and advising clients as they work through difficult employment-related issues. In addition to representing companies, I frequently represent senior executives and professionals in employment matters, usually at the beginning or end of the employment relationship. Among the matters I handle most frequently are cases involving employment contracts, discrimination and harassment claims, wage and hour (overtime) claims, matters involving restrictive covenants (non-competition, non-solicitation, etc.), and whistleblower claims. I work on single-plaintiff cases as well as class actions. I also serve as an arbitrator and mediator. As an arbitrator, my role is to reach a binding decision on the merits after hearing all of the evidence proffered by both parties. If I am selected to serve as a mediator, I facilitate negotiation between the two disputing parties and help them reach a voluntary resolution.

Evaluating an Employment Case

Employment cases cannot be evaluated in a vacuum. Although I have more than two decades of experience representing companies and institutions in various industries, in each new situation my first priority is to learn about the client's business model and goals. Such information is essential for me to assist the client in determining an appropriate strategy. The client's goal is usually to achieve financial success in its business or to achieve a non-profit business goal, and employment disputes—apart from some confidentiality, trade secret, non-competition, and contract claims—routinely distract employers from their day-to-day revenue-generating activities. Most cases, therefore, should be resolved as quickly and cost-effectively as possible.

Although it may seem counterintuitive, the earlier a competent employment lawyer becomes involved in a difficult situation, the more likely it is that a dispute can be avoided or resolved less expensively. Once consulted, I need to make a realistic assessment of where we are in the process. Is the client asking for help before making or carrying out employment decisions, or have the decisions already been made and carried out? Are we talking about one employee or a group? What is the nature of the issue? An employment termination? Violation of a non-compete agreement? An employee disability issue? A complaint of harassment? A demand for overtime pay?

While I can safely assume that maximizing my client's economic interest is a goal, it is also important for me to understand whether there are any non-monetary concerns or values at issue, such as the importance of preserving a particular positive relationship or sending a message to current employees that the company will not respond to frivolous claims. In other words, to what degree are we making decisions based on profit maximization, and to what degree are other concerns involved? Many of the dispute resolution mechanisms in our judicial system are extremely inefficient, costly, and not terribly productive. Therefore, it is usually best if we can find a way to resolve the dispute quickly so my client can go back to doing what it really wants to do—productive work. (Occasionally a party—in my experience, it is more often the employee—pursues litigation because he or she actually enjoys the process. That presents a special set of problems. I try to persuade everyone involved that litigation is unpleasant and unproductive, and ought to be worked through as rapidly and efficiently as possible.)

Preliminary Client Meetings: Questions and Information Gathering

The fact investigation process in an employment dispute, including a complete "download" of the personnel file and documentation leading up to an employee's termination, is often called "internal discovery," and it is extremely important. While much depends upon the point at which I am brought into the process, I have to approach every case as if it will go to trial and gather information based on that assumption. Most employment disputes involve a major change in the employee's circumstances—usually a separation for one reason or another—and I need to know all of the background to that change. I want to know what happened, why it happened, and who the decision-makers were. I want to see all of the documents that led up to the decision, including the entire personnel record and all performance- or discipline-related documents for the employees at issue, as well as similar documents for similarly situated employees who were or are not intended to be affected by the contemplated action. I also want to know as much as possible about the decision-makers and what their history is within the organization, including who they have hired, who they have terminated, what they have done well or poorly, and if there are other complaints against them. In a harassment case, the employer's response to the harassment complaint is very important, and I want to advise the client on how to respond or, if I am retained after the fact, I want to see all of the documentation regarding the employee's complaint and the organization's response.

It is not going to do the client any good if we encounter surprises down the road. I frequently say to the client, "I know you have told me what happened from your perspective, but put yourself in the employee's shoes. What are they going to say, and what is their lawyer going to say? What documents will they want to see?" Fortunately, I often work with human resources professionals who have been on the front lines in the dispute in terms of having had discussions with the employee when the employee was still employed, and they may have done an exit interview as well. They are generally a very good resource with respect to providing me with information about the employee's actions and motivations, and what we can expect from the employee down the road.

Establishing Leverage in an Employment Dispute

I believe it is crucial to establish leverage in an employment dispute as early as possible. The sooner the attorney can gather the facts that establish the value of the case, the better.

The internal discovery discussed above is one key part of establishing leverage. This information provides leverage in various ways. For example, if there is a performance issue, what can we conclusively establish about the plaintiff's performance? We need to know the reason for the termination. Did the plaintiff have a history of poor performance or warnings? Is there some disciplinary issue, or some incident outside of work, that he or she did not tell the client about when he or she applied for employment? If it becomes clear that this information is going to be part of the litigation, will it cause the plaintiff to want to settle? Does anyone at the client company know if the former employee has found new employment yet? Quite often, cases can be resolved quickly if the former employee finds a new job, because an employee's claim for lost wages ends once he or she has found gainful employment.

The second key component of internal discovery is gathering information about the former employee that is not yet in the employer's knowledge. Such information routinely comes from various sources, including researching the employee on the Internet, interviewing individuals outside the company, or using private investigators. Lawyers have to get out from behind their desks in this process and use creativity and common sense to gather information that will provide leverage.

Often in the non-compete area and from time to time in other types of cases, we retain a computer forensic expert to review the former employee's computer to learn what the employee was doing during their tenure with the company besides their work. A tremendous amount of valuable information can be obtained from a properly inspected computer. This information includes evidence that the employee misappropriated the company's information by e-mailing documents, evidence contained in the employee's e-mails that the employee was disloyal to the company, or evidence that the employee deleted or damaged the company's electronic information, potentially violating computer fraud or abuse laws. I inform employers that it is essential that they do not review former employees' computers on their own. It is imperative that a competent forensic expert is retained to ensure electronic evidence is properly preserved and admissible in subsequent litigation.

The third key component of establishing leverage is formal discovery. Once a case is in litigation, I want to take the plaintiff's deposition as soon as possible. Plaintiffs' claims can sometimes be "moving targets," so I want to establish firmly the plaintiff's version of the facts. Typically, prior to taking the plaintiff's deposition, I obtain documents from the employee relating to the claims at issue so I can question the employee about these documents. I also ask a limited number of written questions known as interrogatories to the plaintiff before the deposition to learn about potential witnesses and other basic information. Unchecked, discovery can become overly time-consuming and costly. It is important to maintain focus and discipline to minimize costs and delays.

Simply stated, it is important to establish leverage quickly to resolve disputes in a cost-effective manner.

To Settle or to Litigate

I generally have a pretty good sense of whether an employment dispute will need to be resolved in litigation, or whether there is an opportunity for an early negotiated resolution. In most cases, the more experienced and skilled the lawyer on the other side is, the quicker we can determine whether the case will settle. It is important to get a sense of whether there is some common ground on which we will settle the case—which usually means finding some dollar number range that is going to be mutually acceptable, but might also entail such win-win components as consulting arrangements, investment in the departing employee's new venture, letters of reference, apologies from one side or both, education assistance, in-kind goods or services, or other creative solutions. Conversely, if you are dealing with a less experienced lawyer who is unsure or unrealistic about where the case is going, it may be harder to resolve the dispute early on.

Sometimes an early intervention with a mediator can be very effective, although if either party does not have enough information, you are going to get imperfect results. For example, if the employee claims there is evidence of discrimination or harassment, but has not revealed that evidence, it will be impossible for the employer to credit the employee's evaluation of the case. Experienced counsel or a skilled mediator can often facilitate a rapid informal exchange of information necessary to make a valid evaluation of the claim. In other cases, however, settlement is unlikely until certain key documents have been exchanged and depositions taken, including the plaintiff and the decision-makers.

In many cases, one can assess quickly the value of a case by working with competent opposing counsel and/or a skilled mediator—and if both parties are assessing risks in a rational way, they can typically achieve resolution. I let my clients know that while it may take some time to reach a settlement, it will not take as much time as it does to take depositions and go through a trial. In my own practice, I am litigating cases more efficiently and resolving employment cases earlier now than I was ten years ago, and that is because we know how these cases work and what is likely to happen going forward.

State and Federal Laws and Regulations in Employment Disputes

Employment disputes are governed by a range of state common law and federal, state, and local statutes, depending on whether you are dealing with restrictive covenant (non-competition, non-solicitation, confidential information) cases, wage and hour cases, discrimination cases, whistleblower cases, or business tort or contract cases. Once I know what dispute area the claim falls under—and a single case often involves more than one area—I will consider the applicable statute, regulation, or common law that governs the claim, and think from the beginning about what the summary judgment argument and jury instructions would be if the case was to proceed that far. It is that ultimate application of the law to the facts that governs our assessment of the case—and we focus on it from the beginning.

For example, the prevailing law in restrictive covenant cases is state law. Therefore, the question is which state's law is going to apply to the case—and the answer may not be entirely clear, because the employee may be working in one state but might have an employment agreement that calls for application of the law in another state. Florida, for example, has a statute that governs non-compete agreements, although in most states it is a common law contract issue. California prohibits the use of non-competition agreements in employment, permitting them only in the context of the sale of a business. The status of non-solicitation agreements is unclear in California. The language of the contract will be important as well, in terms of the employee's job description and level in the company. Therefore, when beginning work on a restrictive covenant case, it is important to understand what the contract language actually says and which state law is going to apply to that contract language, keeping in mind that there are many different permutations to consider with respect to the employee's duties and the nature of the client's business. It is also crucial to learn something about the particular court and judges that may be asked to enforce the restrictive covenant, because judges have a lot of discretion in this area.

In discrimination and harassment cases, the law is more uniform and predictable. Federal discrimination law is generally similar to state law, although in some of the larger, more industrialized states the state law is more employee-friendly than the federal law. Discrimination, harassment, and retaliation cases are very fact-driven. Again, thorough internal discovery is key. There are other important statutory areas, such as the Family Medical Leave Act and the many different federal and state whistleblower statutes, where the law is less clearly developed because it has not been around as long. Federal statutes, such as Sarbanes-Oxley, have whistleblower provisions that apply to employees of public companies, particularly with respect to financial accounting issues. Other statutes apply in various regulated industries or to various types of workplace issues. While the attorney must look carefully at the specific provisions of any whistleblower and at the facts alleged, there are many similarities in the structure of these statutes. Typically, to have a claim, the employee must have engaged in "protected conduct," such as complaining about something another employee did that violates the law. The employee must have suffered some adverse employment action, such as a termination or demotion, or even some lesser action. And there must be evidence of a causal relationship between the protected conduct and the adverse employment action.

If we are in the realm of disability or religious discrimination, I want to know what the alleged disability or religious affiliation is and whether the employee requested an accommodation. The term "reasonable accommodation" applies in the areas of disability and religious discrimination, and under some circumstances, the law requires an employer to accommodate an employee's request for special treatment in a certain situation. Examples of religious accommodations include schedule changes to permit Sabbath work prohibitions, or exceptions to dress codes to permit wearing a veil or a yarmulke. Examples of disability accommodations include providing a large-type computer display for an employee with a vision impairment, providing a leave of absence for an employee who needs chemotherapy, and changing a work schedule for an employee who needs to go to Alcoholics Anonymous meetings. It is important to keep in mind that the assessment of whether an employee has a "disability" under the law and whether a particular accommodation is "reasonable" depends on the facts of a particular case.

Financial Considerations

As with most business and legal decisions, cost/benefit analysis is key in employment cases. It is always important to perform a probability risk analysis of an employment case (i.e., what is the likelihood of getting the results the client wants). If I know there is a 50 percent chance of the client having to pay the other party $100,000 and it is going to cost $50,000 to $100,000 to get to that verdict, is litigation worth it? Those are all important pieces of data I need to give to the client to assist the client in deciding whether to go to trial or settle.

Consequently, it is also necessary to consider the potential damages in an employment dispute, along with the even harder to quantify costs of lost time on the part of the executives who have to devote their attention to the case. It is important to consider the distraction factor of litigation, and the actual number of days the client's managers will have to spend dealing with the case instead of spending time on revenue-generating work for the company. The client's legal fees, including any expert witness and computer forensics costs, also factor into the cost/benefit analysis.

Of course, there is also some cost to settling in terms of the risk of emboldening other employees to make similar claims. The likelihood of settlement causing employees to "jump on the bandwagon" depends on the nature of the company, the individual plaintiff at issue, and the circumstances of the case. I find a very wide variation among clients in terms of how this factor is gauged. In some situations, the risk of settlement with respect to inviting similar lawsuits is a very real concern, and the cost of going to trial is well worth the expense, while in others it is less significant. As an example, take a company that establishes a reduction-in-force process and a severance pay policy that applies to a large group of similarly situated employees. If one of those employees sues seeking a payment greater than the severance offered, it may be important for the company to make clear that it intends to win that case at trial, because settlement could lead to large numbers of similar claims. On the other hand, if one employee is terminated for performance reasons, and files a lawsuit, there may be no significant likelihood that settling with that person will result in future claims by others.

The Value of Mediation

I have found that mediation in an employment dispute will only work if both parties are willing to consider settlement. Some courts have mandatory mediation, which can be helpful in some cases simply because there is often value in getting both parties together in the same room. In some cases, an employer-run mediation program is designed to resolve disputes between two parties, both of whom are employed by the company, or between the company and a current employee. Mediation may also arise in a situation where the plaintiff has already been terminated and he or she is making a claim through an administrative agency or in court.

Mediation is more likely to be effective in some cases than in others. For example, if an employee with a disability makes a complaint but remains employed, early mediation or negotiation can be especially helpful in resolving disputes about reasonable accommodations. Monetary disputes can be harder to settle, particularly if one party has unrealistic expectations. Therefore, as noted above, counsel should approach every case as if it will go to trial. Because mediation is about compromise, it is unlikely to result in one party obtaining a huge settlement that will provide for financial independence or some type of public vindication or an admission of guilt. On the other hand, if the client's goal is some sort of reasonable financial assistance, a private apology, or a limited time consulting arrangement (i.e., a more modest and obtainable goal), mediation is much more likely to work. A good mediator can help bring the parties' expectations to a more realistic level as a step toward resolving the dispute. In some cases though, one or both parties may need the time and procedures of a litigation process, including depositions or even a trial, to reach a resolution.

Conclusion

Employment disputes involve issues that mean a lot to people—their livelihood, their identity, and their hope for the future. The growth of legal protections for employees over the last twenty-five years has created numerous grounds for employees to mount legal challenges to employer action. These challenges can become very costly to employers in terms of either legal fees or settlement payments. To effectively resolve these disputes, an attorney must not only know the law, but he or she must effectively and efficiently gather information that will enable the client to make an informed decision as to whether to proceed to trial or settle.

Douglas T. Schwarz leads Bingham McCutchen LLP's New York labor and employment group. He represents public and private companies and not-for-profit institutions in matters concerning all aspects of labor and employment law. He tries cases and argues appeals in federal and state courts, in arbitrations, and before administrative agencies. He also serves as an arbitrator and mediator. He also represents clients in a range of other discrimination matters, including housing, education, and public accommodations discrimination cases, and cases involving accessibility under the Americans with Disabilities Act and state and local law.

Mr. Schwarz has served in government as commissioner of the Massachusetts Commission against Discrimination, a role in which he oversaw the investigation of claims of discrimination, mediated discrimination disputes, adjudicated cases at public hearings, and led numerous policy initiatives. He also served as an assistant attorney general in the civil rights division of the Massachusetts Office of the Attorney General, and as a law clerk to the Honorable Franklin S. Billings Jr. of the U.S. District Court for the District of Vermont.

Mr. Schwarz is admitted to practice in Massachusetts and New York. He earned his B.A. from Dartmouth College and his J.D. from Harvard Law School.

The Role of the Mediator in Resolving Employment Disputes

J. Randall Patterson

Shareholder

Baker Donelson Bearman Caldwell & Berkowitz PC

ASPATORE

The Nature of Employment Disputes

As an employment lawyer, I have the unique opportunity to view employment disputes from an outside analytical or third-party perspective. While most employment disputes arise in the context of a termination or from a decision that frustrates an employee's ambition, I have observed that many such disputes are the product of miscommunication or misunderstood expectations. As a general rule, if employees (and people in general) understand what is expected of them, it is human nature, at least superficially, to want to do a good job and succeed. With that said, most employers do a reasonable job of communicating their expectations to their employees. Problems most often arise when employees do not comprehend exactly what the employer expects of them or when they have pre-conceived ideas about what their job should be, or both. Because of this, I believe that as a threshold matter, it is crucial that companies have effective and well-written handbooks and policy statements in place. I also advise my clients to conduct and require attendance at in-depth orientation programs for all new employees. It is advisable to also have follow-up sessions that conduct refresher training for existing employees as well as managers on those policies and handbooks on a regular basis. I also encourage my clients to have their policies and handbooks reviewed annually, and to introduce or "roll out" those new updated handbooks or policies with in-house training sessions. These in-house training sessions, in my opinion, achieve the optimum results when conducted in two separate modules: one for management with a focus on litigation prevention, the other for the general workforce with a focus on policies the employer has adopted to ensure equal opportunity and employee rights in the workplace, and how all employees have an affirmative duty to report harassing, discriminative, or otherwise unlawful conduct. Taking these steps helps solidify and ensure an employer's expectations of employees, and helps the workforce better understand the employer's expectations of them more clearly.

It has been my experience that employment disputes are some of the most difficult matters to resolve. As a new lawyer, I did some domestic relations work, and having practiced now for almost twenty years, next to those family law cases, employment matters are probably the most personal and emotionally charged type of litigation. I think this is because most people generally draw their self-esteem, at least to some degree, from their job or the work they do, and often their particular employment position itself. When that is threatened or terminated, it is usually taken as very personal by the affected employee. Because of this, employment cases are different from typical commercial litigation disputes, because the motivating factor of commercial disputes is usually financial. That is not to say financial factors do not play an enormous part in employment cases as well, but the additional personal or emotional element of an employment matter often makes settlement of that type of case more challenging.

Another part of my law practice involves the mediation of disputes. In that role, which is very different from that of an advocate, I try to remind the parties involved that the purpose of mediation is not to draw venom, but to simply resolve the dispute. It is also important in mediation that the parties understand they are not there to convince the mediator of the merits of their case. As I tell parties when I am mediating a case, as long as they are talking to each other, my day is easy. My job as a neutral is not to make decisions or provide legal advice. My role is that of a compromise and settlement facilitator. There is nothing particularly glorious in that fact, but the idea is simply to keep the parties talking and treating each other with respect. The mediator's task is simply to direct the parties back to the relevant issues if they should stray away from them, and to point out the strengths and weaknesses of the case that, for whatever reason, may not have been recognized or acknowledged.

Important Laws and Regulations

The law with which I deal most often in my multi-state litigation practice is Title VII, which of course prohibits discrimination based on race and gender in the workplace. I have also noticed that recently there seems to be a greater number of religious discrimination claims being filed, along with a few equal pay claims. Other actions that seem to consistently be filed are those arising under the Americans with Disabilities Act.

In working through an employment dispute, laws other than just the federal statutes must be considered. Wrongful termination claims, sounding under state law, are often pendant to such federal claims. For example, Mississippi is a state where its jurisprudence has embraced the "employment at will" doctrine for more than 150 years, but there are some common-law, or case-created, carve-outs to that at-will doctrine. For example, one exception to the at-will doctrine may arise from policies and employment terms contained in an employer's handbook. That carve-out essentially requires that if an employer creates a policy, such as a progressive discipline policy with various steps that have to be implemented before an employee can be terminated, and then provides that policy to its employees so they rely upon it, the courts are going to "hold the employer to its word."[1] Courts have consistently held that if an employer puts such policies in their handbooks, they are going to have to follow them to the letter when they discipline or terminate an employee. It is important to note that the courts have been clear that this exception to the at-will doctrine does not purport to create a greater tenure, or right to employment. It simply requires that the employer follow its own outlined steps when taking adverse action against an employee.

Another common exception to the at-will doctrine that should be kept in mind is known as a public policy exception, commonly called a whistleblower exception. This type of exception routinely provides that an at-will employee cannot be terminated for refusing to engage in an "illegal act," or for reporting an "illegal act." [2] This evolving exception has been the subject of much litigation over the last few years, particularly concerning the definition of what conduct actually constitutes an "illegal act" for purposes of this legal theory. A Mississippi state appellate court recently determined that an illegal act for purposes of the whistleblower exception to the at-will doctrine must be a violation of a statute that would carry a criminal sanction, as opposed to a civil sanction. While such decisions provide some guidance for this southern state, every jurisdiction is going to have variations of its at-will exceptions that should be thoroughly researched when responding to a claim of retaliatory discharge.

A Strategic Approach to Employment Dispute Resolution

As addressed above, there are generally two roles I may assume in approaching a labor or employment dispute. That role is, of course, defined by what I have been hired or appointed to do. The first and most traditional role is, of course, that of advocate. As litigators, we assume the role of

[1] *Bobbit vs. Orchard*, LTD, 603 So.2d 356 (Miss. 1992).
[2] *McArn v. Allied Bruce Terminex Company Inc.*, 626 So.2d 603 (Miss. 1993).

advocate in any dispute involving actual litigation. Of course, this role requires counsel to represent the interest of his or her client, and to make efforts to bring about a desirable result within the confines of ethical behavior and practices and the rules of court. Alternatively, the role I play as a mediator or neutral is very different from that of advocate. As a neutral, I do not assume a position on behalf of either party, and I consciously work to maintain that non-biased posture throughout the mediation. In mediation, the collective goal should be to effectively communicate the conflicting positions of the two parties to each other, in hopes of the parties reaching an agreement to resolve their dispute. The mediator decides nothing. If the dispute settles, it is because the parties agree for it to do so. In the case of arbitration, the neutral's role is somewhat different and he or she serves, much like a judge, as a decision-maker or fact-finder. In that context, he or she listens objectively to the positions of the advocates, considers the evidence presented, and assigns a finding. The parties to arbitration, much like traditional litigants, defer the decision of how their dispute will be resolved to a third party.

Key Documentation

It has been my experience that while employment law matters are not typically document-intensive, the documents involved in the dispute are usually critical to a favorable outcome. The documents required by me to evaluate a matter vary depending on the details of that particular case. From the perspective of an advocate, necessary documents generally include those that are provided through the course of internal fact-finding, pre-discovery disclosures, and routine discovery. From the very different perspective of a neutral mediating an employment case, it is required that the advocate counsel submit a brief mediation position statement that provides an overview of the case and candidly discusses the strengths and weaknesses that are perceived within the case. It is also helpful for the parties to provide an honest appraisal of their position with regard to settlement. This information puts the mediator in a better position for guiding those parties through meaningful settlement discussions. In such mediations, the position statements are provided in confidence and are not exchanged between the parties. The contents of the position statements, as well as information provided to the mediator during the conference, is typically treated as confidential, apart from a waiver or consent to disclose by the parties.

Mediations

Traditional labor law deals with labor relations usually in the union context, collective bargaining, and National Labor Relations Board matters, and the procedure in handling such matters is typically dictated in the terms of the relevant collective bargaining agreement. Employment law mediation is very different and has more to do with issues arising under statutory or common law. In mediating an employment dispute, the parties' confidential mediation position statement should be provided well in advance of the actual mediation conference. The conference should be scheduled in a place where both sides are comfortable. An ideal conference location would have a primary meeting or conference room and at least two break-out or caucus rooms where the parties might go for private discussions. The availability of two similar rooms is important, because if there is only one, there is an obvious question of which party stays and which party is required to move. Ideally, both parties will have identical facilities.

Another consideration that should be addressed early on is payment of mediation expenses. It is my opinion that the costs of mediation should be born equally by the parties. Such equal division alleviates any appearance of impropriety—that the mediator is being paid for by one of the parties. Secondly, and just as important, is the fact that if parties are economically investing in the mediation, they will more likely come to that conference with a more realistic and good faith willingness to work toward resolution of the claim. An economic investment in the process, I believe, motivates the parties to really try to negotiate in good faith and use best efforts to settle the claim. Without that financial investment, parties may agree to participate just to get a look at their opponent's case, without really being there to settle the case.

My experience is that the typical mediation conference begins with everyone together. Each party has the opportunity to make a brief opening statement—not to the mediator, but to the other party. After opening statements, the parties will typically break into separate sessions, and the mediator should strive to spend equal periods of time with each side discussing the merits of the case and conveying settlement offers until, hopefully, there is some kind of conciliation.

A successful mediation conference usually concludes with parties coming back together in a joint session. The mediator may have a standard settlement he or she uses, or they may, as I do, ask a volunteer to write up the mediation settlement agreement. As a mediator, I prefer the parties to do this rather than me. Once the agreement is reduced to writing, each party should sign, acknowledging that these are the terms that have been agreed upon. As a general rule, I destroy the original document and each party, as well as myself, leave with an identical copy of the agreement.

Also, when the mediation conference is concluded either by settlement or impasse, the mediator often will destroy all of his or her personal notes from that conference. When I mediate a matter, I require the parties to sign a mediation agreement prior to the beginning of the conference. Pertinent parts of most such agreements require that the parties treat each other with respect, that they are at the conference to negotiate in good faith, and that what is said in the conference will remain confidential. As a mediator, I only disclose exactly what the parties ask me to disclose. Should the mediation conference not be successful, then as part of my agreement, the parties consent that I cannot be subpoenaed as a witness. Finally, I require that everyone acknowledge there are no documents to be subpoenaed from me, because as mentioned above, they will all be destroyed at the conclusion of the conference. I have found that this process facilitates candor as well as more open communications, and of course precludes me being later compelled to respond to a subpoena.

At the outset of the conference, I try to put the burden on the parties to educate me on the issues of the case or dispute. This can be accomplished through the submission of pre-conference mediation position statements along with any documents the parties would like to present, or by an opening statement, or both.

Achieving a Successful Outcome

As an initial matter, there are important financial considerations to encourage reaching resolution of a matter through mediation. From a plaintiff's standpoint, time seems to be the most valuable commodity. Conversely, from a corporate defendant employer, the cost of defense counsel seems to be the primary motivating factor. Litigation of an employment case can be expensive, and more often than not resolution through the court takes a long time. Because of these motivating factors, a good mediator will remind the parties of a simple fact: that when a party chooses to litigate, there is no quick or cheap resolution. Additionally, when litigation is chosen as a means of conflict resolution, the outcome of that very important matter is not placed in the hands of a third party, the judge, or a jury, to decide. There have been "slam dunk" cases that should have been won, but were lost, and vice versa, and anytime a case goes to court, while outcomes may be somewhat predictable, the judge or jury are always wild cards. There are always unforeseen factors that could sway the direction in which a case is decided in court. Parties considering mediation services should be reminded that through mediation they have the unique opportunity to actually decide the problem themselves, and that it is not necessary to put these important decisions in the hands of a third-party judge, jury, or arbitrator. Rather, through mediation, the parties can communicate freely, directly with each other, and hopefully, work together toward terms and settlement or solution that everyone can accept.

Fostering Excellent Client Relationships

Most lawyers by nature have competitive, over-achieving personalities. Because of this, it is sometimes easy to approach a litigation matter as some sort of competition rather than a business dispute, with resolution as a goal rather than defeat of the opposing side. We, as litigators, must keep in mind that we are not engaging in a sporting event for our own gratification. We are representing the real interests of a party, and often those interests are not served by posturing for the sake of competition with opposing counsel. It is important to remember that in most cases the party's true interest is in resolving the case and moving on. My advice to other employment litigators would be, as difficult as it is sometimes, to put the interest of the clients ahead of your own urge to be a gladiator, and to work toward a prompt and economical resolution of the matter, even if there is no doubt in your mind that you could soundly defeat your opponent. The decision to settle, of course, always belongs to the client.

Client relations in a mediation practice is somewhat unique, and is very different from in a normal litigation practice, in that parties come to see the mediator, usually only once. While there may be repeat requests for mediation services in various matters, these parties are not clients in the traditional sense. These parties are retaining the mediator to help them resolve a case, often on a one-time basis.

Conversely, in building relationships with my existing long-term clients, it is crucial to recognize that clients generally do not hire law firms. They hire lawyers. Even the largest corporations need confidence in that individual face associated with who they are hiring, so I make a point of maintaining a personal relationship with the clients for whom I do regular work, and I make an effort to visit them at least annually, no matter where their offices are located. I also try to stay abreast of their particular industry, services, or product. If it is a restaurant, I want to know where they are opening new stores, and how those stores are doing. If it is an insurance company, I want to know what lines of coverage they are selling, and I try to meet the new adjustors and team leaders. With construction clients, I want to know what projects they are currently working on, as well as the problems they are experiencing beyond the narrow area of labor and employment. Taking time to get to know your clients is key. Attempting to understand the client's particular segment of the industry helps build long-term and successful relationships.

When employment litigation arises, an ideal client will have adequate documentation to support any challenged decision. If it is a long-term client, we probably wrote their handbook and policies. This compliance type of work is positive for client development. It is also a good idea to be active in national, regional, and local seminars that are geared to educate employers on how to avoid litigation and how to best defend when confronted with a problem. Such seminars may be done through local chambers of commerce or industry associations. Additionally, as discussed above, in-house training for long-term clients on issues such as discrimination or harassment complaints may prove determinative later when they are defending a lawsuit.

In a healthy client relationship, the client's expectations of me and my expectations of that client need to be transparent. By that, I mean it is critical for clients to understand that while I am "their lawyer," I also have many other clients. While I will make every effort to be available and will be in contact as much as possible, an expectation of availability all day every day is unrealistic, and often results in frustration. If a client has an emergency, I do not mean to suggest it will not be serviced in a timely fashion. It certainly will, but it is necessary for clients to understand that the lawyer is not theirs exclusively. One point that must be stressed is attorney responsiveness. If I am unavailable, my client's issue or problem will be timely addressed, and I will personally follow up with that client as soon as possible.

One expectation I have of clients is that of absolute truthfulness, and one expectation they should have of me is absolute candor. With the complete information provided by the client, it is then my job to provide their legal options so they might make an informed decision. I do not always expect clients to hear everything I say the first time, and in most cases I am going to come back again and maybe say it another way. If they have engaged in a poor or improper practice, and have exposure in a matter, I am going to explain those risks. Clients make business decisions rather than legal decisions, so from that perspective I am going to advise the client of the probable outcomes based on various decision alternatives. Then I will ask them what they want to do, based on their business goals and those probable outcomes. But again, honesty is the most essential element of a successful client relationship. I do not want a client failing to disclose information that puts me in a precarious situation with other attorneys or the court. What clients can expect from me is excellent service, absolute dedication, reasonable availability (e.g., returning their phone call within twenty-four hours, without exception), and excellent representation.

The Benefits of a Proactive Approach

The best strategy for addressing employment problems is preventive action. A handbook that includes policies that provide every potential defense is critical. It is also necessary to have a good orientation program that effectively trains all employees. We have won several hostile work environment cases asserting the *Ellerth/Faragher* [3] defense. This defense is effective where the employer has a sound policy prohibiting anti-discrimination or anti-harassment, and a policy that requires employees to

[3] *Faragher v. City of Boca Raton*, 524 U.S. 775 (1998); *Burlington Indus. Inc. v. Ellerth*, 524 U.S. 742 (1998).

report suspected conduct that violates that policy. If the employees are trained and still fail to take advantage of those preventative measures, that failure is their responsibility, and liability cannot generally be imputed to the employer.

My advice to clients is to make sure their employee handbook is a good one, train their people on it, and train them consistently and regularly. Put in place an excellent orientation program, and document everything. If you have a bad employee, make sure the performance evaluations or write-ups are accurate. Effective documentation requires training supervisors and managers on how to create proper documentation and evaluations—without this training, their records will be erratic, and they will probably therefore appear to be discriminatory. The key to a successful defense of employment-related claims is preparation through documentation.

J. Randall Patterson is a shareholder in Baker, Donelson, Bearman, Caldwell & Berkowitz's Jackson, Mississippi office. He concentrates his litigation practice on the areas of labor and employment law. He devotes a significant amount of his practice to representing employers before the Equal Employment Opportunity Commission and in defending lawsuits related to harassment or discrimination in the workplace. He frequently consults with employers on labor issues, and he has written or revised many employee handbooks.

Appendices

APPENDIX A

CHECKLIST OF ISSUES TO BE CONSIDERED IN A PLANT CLOSURE/MASS LAYOFF

A. WARN

1. Is the company subject to the notice requirements of the Worker Adjustment and Retraining Notification Act?

   a. Does the company employ 100 or more full-time employees?

   b. Does the company employ 100 or more employees, including part-time employees, who work a total of at least 4000 hours per week, excluding overtime?

   c. Have all employees working 20 hours or more per week, and six or more of the preceding twelve months, been counted as full-time employees?

2. Is the employee being laid off as the result of a "plant closing"?

   a. Is there a permanent or temporary shutdown of a single site of employment, or one or more facilities or operating units within a site?

   b. Will the shutdown result in 50 or more full-time employees being out of work during a 30 day period?

   c. In determining whether there has been a plant closing, have all closings within 90 days been considered in the aggregate?

3. Is the employee being laid off as the result of a "mass layoff"?

   a. Does the reduction in the company's workforce result in an employment loss at a single site for 50 or more full-time employees and affect at least one-third of the full-time workforce at the site?

b. Does the reduction in the company's workforce result in an employment loss at a single site for 500 or more full-time employees?

c. In determining whether there has been a mass layoff, have all reductions in the workforce occurring within 90 days been considered in the aggregate?

4. Have all employment losses been considered?

a. Employment terminations, other than a discharge for cause, voluntary departure, or retirement?

b. Layoffs exceeding six months?

c. Reductions in hours of more than 50 percent during each month of a six month period?

5. Have all appropriate parties been provided with 60 days' notice?

a. All non-union employees, except those hired on a temporary basis, who may reasonably be expected to experience an employment loss?

b. All nonunion employees whose jobs will be eliminated or who may be displaced due to bumping rights?

c. All appropriate representatives of unionized employees?

d. The state's dislocated worker unit?

e. The local government within which the closing or layoff is to occur?

6. May the company provide less than 60 days' notice of its plant closings due to efforts to obtain capital or business?

a. Was the company actively seeking capital or business at the time the 60 day notice would have been required?

b. Was there a realistic opportunity to obtain the financing or business sought?

c. Would the capital or business sought, if obtained, enable the company to avoid or postpone the plant closing for a reasonable period of time?

d. Did the company reasonably and in good faith believe that giving notice would have precluded it from obtaining the needed capital or business?

7. May the company provide less than 60 days' notice of its plant closing or mass layoff due to unforeseeable business circumstances?

a. Was the unforeseeable business circumstance caused by some "sudden, dramatic, and unexpected" action outside the company's control?

b. May the company avoid providing 60 days' notice of its plant closing or mass layoff due to a strike or lockout?

B. COBRA

1. Is the company subject to the requirements of the Consolidated Omnibus Budget Reconciliation Act?

2. Has administrative responsibility for compliance with COBRA been determined and assigned (i.e., is the insurance carrier or the company going to be responsible for mandated notices, administration, etc.)?

a. Does the company normally employ 20 or more employees?

b. Has the company employed at least 20 or more employees on at least 50 percent of the company's working days during the preceding calendar year?

c. Is the company a successor employer which has continued the operations and workforce of its predecessor?

3. Does the company maintain a group health care plan which is established to provide medical care to employees, former employees or their families?

4. Have all qualified "beneficiaries" been provided the benefit of continued coverage?

a. Covered employees who are terminated, either voluntarily or involuntarily?

b. Covered employees whose hours of work are reduced such that they are no longer entitled to coverage?

c. The spouse and dependent children of such covered employees?

d. Independent contractors, partners, and self-employed individuals provided coverage by virtue of the performance of services?

5. Has the company provided the appropriate period of continuation coverage?

a. Eighteen months of continued coverage for termination or reduction in hours.

b. Thirty-six months for death, divorce; legal separation, cessation of a child's dependent status, or Medicare entitlement.

6. Is the continuation coverage identical to coverage provided to similarly situated active plan participants and their beneficiaries?

7. Has the qualified beneficiary been provided 60 days to initially elect continuation coverage?

8. Do the premiums for continuation coverage equal 102 percent or less than the premium paid by active beneficiaries (or 150 percent or less for those eligible for the 29-month disability extension)?

9. Has the qualified beneficiary been provided the appropriate opportunity to pay for continuation coverage?

a. Has the qualified beneficiary been allowed to pay for continuation coverage in monthly installments?

b. Has the qualified beneficiary been provided with a grace period to pay for continuation coverage?

c. Has the beneficiary been allowed to make the initial premium within 45 days within the date of election?

10. Has the company provided timely notice to the plan administrator of the appropriate qualifying event?

C. FINAL WAGES

1. Has the employee been laid off or discharged?

a. Have all earned and unpaid wages been paid "immediately"?

b. Have the final wages been paid at the place of discharge?

2. Has the employee resigned from employment not covered by a written contract for a definite term?

a. If the employee has given less than 72 hours notice of his or her intention to quit, have the final wages been paid within 72 hours?

b. If the employee has given 72 or more hours notice of his or her intention to quit, have the final wages been paid at the time of quitting?

c. Have the final wages been paid at the office or agency in the county where the employee worked?

3. If there is a dispute as to the total wages due, have all wages or portions thereof conceded to be due been paid?

4. Have all vested and unused vacation and other paid leave benefits been included in the employee's final paycheck?

a. Have all such benefits been calculated consistent with the company's policy or practice and prorated where appropriate?

b. Have all forfeitures of vested benefits been avoided?

5. Have all commissions been included in the employee's final paycheck?

a. Have the commissions been calculated consistent with the terms of the commission agreement?

b. Does the commission agreement clearly specify when commissions are earned, when paid, and the consequences of a termination of employment?

c. Have all forfeitures of vested commissions been avoided?

6. Have there been any deductions or set offs from the employee's final paycheck?

a. Have the deductions been made as a result of a dishonest or willful act or the culpable negligence of the employee, and not as a result of losses due to simple negligence?

b. Is there sufficient evidence to satisfy the company's burden of proof that deductions were based upon a dishonest or willful act or the culpable negligence of the employee?

c. Have the deductions been made pursuant to the employee's written authorization for indebtedness resulting from a loan, product purchase, educational assistance or similar advancement?

D. ERISA

1. Have all employee benefit plan documents been reviewed to determine employer duties and obligations upon plan participant (i.e., employee) termination?

2. Have plan documents and employer formal and informal policies been reviewed to determine if any employee benefits plans are "ERISA plans"?

3. Have ERISA reporting and disclosure provisions for all ERISA employee benefit plans been complied with?

4. Has the "administrator" responsible for plan notices and reporting been identified, and has responsibility for ERISA compliance been clearly assigned?

5. Has the proposed number of terminating pension plan participants been reviewed to determine if the layoff constitutes a termination or partial termination of the pension plan, as defined in ERISA?

    a. If a partial termination or full plan termination will or may occur as a result of the layoff, has the plan administrator and/or legal counsel been contacted to determine the effect of termination or partial termination on the vesting of benefits and increased reporting and disclosure requirements?

    b. Has the cost of premature vesting caused by a termination or partial termination been determined, and has liability for the increased cost been established?

    c. If the employer participates in a multi-employer pension plan, has it been determined whether the layoff will trigger a plan withdrawal, and has withdrawal liability been estimated?

6. Have terminated employees been given all ERISA-mandated notices regarding vested benefits, including summary plan descriptions and "material" modifications, as well as summary annual reports?

    a. Have individual employees made all necessary elections?

b. Have mechanisms been created to prove that all required notices have been provided?

7. Has a mechanism that complies with ERISA been established for accepting benefit claims, and for handling appeals from the denial of claims?

a. Is responsibility for handling and responding to claims established?

b. Are the ERISA timelines for responding to claims understood, and has a mechanism been established to ensure their observance?

8. Has the required tax implication notice been provided to terminating plan participants receiving pension plan distributions?

9. Has there been compliance with COBRA notice provisions for all terminating medical plan participants? (See COBRA checklist.)

10. Have other welfare benefit plan documents been reviewed to determine if terminating plan participants are entitled to conversion rights?

11. Has the potential for "negative inferences" regarding the motive for the layoff been considered, particularly where the layoff will divest large numbers of employees of ERISA benefits, or prevent their vesting, or will yield an unexpected "windfall" to the employer?

E. WORKERS' COMPENSATION

1. Have "problem" employees on or recently returning from workers' compensation disability leaves been identified, and has their selection for "layoff" been reviewed to determine vulnerability to discrimination claims?

2. Have you designated those persons among your personnel to whom work-related injuries or illness are to be promptly reported? Most employers use first line management (i.e., foreman, supervisors).

3. Have you instructed in advance the foremen or supervisors so designated regarding the information which employees must report and

which the foremen and supervisors must document? At the very least this includes the date, time and place of injury, name, occupation and signature of the injured employee, how the injury occurred and whether there were any witnesses to the accident causing the injury.

4. Have you maintained and publicized a policy requiring employees to report any work-related injuries or illnesses to designated personnel immediately?

5. Have you investigated each claim thoroughly and immediately upon receiving notice of a claim?

 a. Have you enlisted your insurance carrier's assistance in this regard?

 b. Have you identified and interviewed all witnesses?

 c. Have you maintained up-to-date information regarding the addresses and telephone numbers of witnesses who are subsequently terminated?

6. Have you established in advance the liaison persons between the insurance carrier or claims administrator and the employer?

7. Have you promptly notified the insurance carrier or claims administrator regarding the injury?

 a. Did you call immediately upon receiving notice or knowledge of an injury to advise the claims adjuster of the potential claim and send the Employee's Claim for Workers' Compensation Benefits (for injuries occurring on or after January 1, 1990), the Employer's Report of Occupational Injury or Illness and any additional information in your possession regarding the claim?

 b. Did your insurer/claims administrator accept or reject the claim within the 90 days required (for injuries occurring on or after January 1, 1990)?

c. Have you contacted your insurer or claims administrator regarding acceptance or rejection of the claim prior to the expiration of the 90 day period?

d. Have you provided your insurer/claims administrator with all the information in your possession which may help refute liability?

8. Have you determined in advance where medical treatment will be obtained for industrially injured employees?

a. Where possible, have you immediately taken control of medical treatment by directing the injured employee to the designated medical care provider for treatment?

b. Have you contracted with a particular medical clinic, hospital or doctor for the furnishing of immediate medical care or treatment?

F. EEO CONSIDERATIONS

1. Has the scope of the layoff been determined?

a. What are the projected post-layoff staffing requirements?

b. Any openings in other departments or divisions?

c. Have current job functions been analyzed?

d. Have current employee work skills been determined?

2. Have appropriate nondiscriminatory selection criteria been adopted?

a. Does the selection criteria provide sufficient flexibility so that the most productive employees are retained?

b. Is the selection criteria sufficiently objective and job-related?

c. Does the selection criteria intentionally discriminate against members of a protected group?

3. Do the selection criteria adversely impact a protected group?

a. Has a projected layoff list been generated?

b. Does the layoff affect 20 or more employees?

c. Has the workforce been reviewed to determine the percentage of individuals in protected classifications?

d. Does the proposed layoff result in a statistical disparity which is considered legally significant?

4. Have those employees selected for layoff been properly notified?

a. Has management conducted exit interviews?

b. Have employees been informed of the selection criteria adopted and the specific reason for their layoff?

5. Despite a disparate impact, will the layoff withstand judicial scrutiny?

a. Is the layoff economically justified?

b. Do the selection criteria serve a legitimate business interest?

c. Has inside or outside counsel reviewed the selection criteria and underlying business justification?

d. Are there any other possible legal defenses to a potential discrimination claim?

6. In evaluating which employees are to be laid off, have the merits of giving "extra credit" to older workers been weighed?

G. EARLY RETIREMENT AND SEVERANCE PROGRAMS

1. Is there a plan to offer early retirement or severance incentives in advance of or in conjunction with a layoff?

2. If it is planned to seek volunteers for early retirement, will the plan avoid presenting layoff or demotion as the alternative?

3. Have retirement-eligible employees been offered benefits under any severance plans irrespective of their eligibility for retirement benefits?

4. If there has been an attempt to integrate retirement and severance benefits, have the limitations of the Older Workers' Benefit Protection Act been observed?

   a. Have deductions from the amount of severance benefits been limited to amounts permitted by OWBPA?

5. If a release or severance agreement is being sought which will waive any rights or claims arising under the Age Discrimination in Employment Act, have the requirements of the OWBPA been observed?

   a. Is the agreement in writing, and understandable to the employee?

   b. Does the agreement specifically refer to rights under the ADEA?

   c. Are any waivers limited to present, as opposed to future, rights?

   d. Is the individual receiving additional "consideration" for the waiver?

   e. Has the individual been advised, in writing, to consult a lawyer?

   f. Has the individual been given sufficient time to consider the agreement?

g. Where an individual is entering the agreement as part of a group or class of employees participating in an "exit incentive" or "early retirement" program, has all required information been provided to the employee in writing?

H. LAYOFF PROCEDURES

1. Have employment contracts, personnel policies, employee manuals, application forms or business practices in any way limited the company's freedom to lay off employees?

a. Is there a formal or informal discipline system?

b. Have employee performance deficiencies been honestly reviewed prior to any layoffs?

c. Are current and past employee evaluations consistent with the stated reasons for performance-based layoffs?

d. Have employees subject to layoff been given, explicitly or implicitly, any "bumping" or transfer rights?

2. Where layoffs are conducted on the basis of performance, is the employer prepared to explain and defend the decision in response to individual employee inquiries?

a. Can the employer explain how laid off employees' responsibilities will be handled after the layoff?

b. Can the employer explain and reconcile the layoff with current and projected manpower requirements?

3. Has the employer reviewed and clarified its own policies with respect to accrued but unused vacation, holiday, sick pay, and PTO in the event of a layoff?

4. Have policies regarding "seniority," breaks in "seniority" and recall been adopted, reviewed or clarified?

a. Have such policies been disclosed to employees?

5. Has the company complied with the terms of any collective bargaining agreements it has with labor unions?

a. With respect to the right to lay off employees?

b. With respect to layoff procedures?

c. With respect to any restrictions on the "subcontracting" of bargaining unit work?

6. Has the employer satisfied its "duty to bargain" with any labor unions representing its employees?

7. Have all contingent liabilities (i.e., vacation, holiday, sick pay, severance pay) under union contracts been reviewed and calculated?

8. Have the merits of decentralized versus centralized administration of the layoff been weighed?

9. Have the merits of successive layoffs rather than a single layoff been weighed?

10. Has a uniform layoff or termination message been prepared?

a. Have the number of employer representatives authorized to discuss the layoff been limited, and are the authorized representatives fully briefed on all aspects of the layoff (i.e., reasons, duration, employee eligibility for transfer or recall)?

11. Are employer representatives announcing the layoff prepared to answer employee questions?

12. Has the public spokesman on the layoff been designated, and has a review procedure for public statements been established?

13. Are employer representatives familiar with public and private outplacement assistance and other benefits available to laid off employees?

a. Do the employer representatives know where to refer employees with specific benefit questions?

14. Where severance payments are to be provided, are they spread out over a period of time?

15. Where employees are allowed to "volunteer" for layoff, have the unemployment compensation consequences been recognized and explained to employees?

16. Have all appropriate ADEA, EEO, DFEH and IWC notices been properly posted?

17. Have security needs been evaluated, and are the procedures established commensurate with legitimate needs?

18. If not dictated by WARN, the OWBPA, employer policies or a collective bargaining agreement, has the notice period in advance of the layoff been determined, and is the notice period reasonable?

I. MISCELLANEOUS

1. Have "problem" employees (i.e., "whistle blowers," pregnant and disabled employees, threatened litigants, and those who have made "protected" complaints about health, safety or union organization) scheduled for layoff been identified, and have steps been taken to ensure that the layoff decision can be justified with respect to those employees?

2. Have limitations imposed by state and federal law upon the termination of reservists called to active duty been observed?

3. Have those employees been identified as to whom representations regarding tenure were made, and has liability to such employees under Labor Code Sections 970 and 972 been considered and evaluated?

4. Have steps been taken to secure the assignment of employee inventions consistent with California Labor Code Sections 2870-72?

5. Have steps been taken to protect trade secrets and prevent unfair competition or the solicitation of valued employees?

   a. Have enforceable unfair competition provisions been included in any severance agreement?

b. Have any restrictive covenants been reasonably limited in scope, duration and geographic extent?

c. Are "trade secrets" protected by any severance agreement really "trade secrets," and has the laid off employee been provided with any "independent consideration" to support secrecy agreements?

6. Have employer tax liabilities for severance pay been recognized and accounted for?

7. If a union represents employees, the employer has a host of additional considerations including bargaining over the decision and/or the effects of the decision

Courtesy of Chris Baker, Thelen Reid Brown Raysman & Steiner LLP

APPENDIX B

SAMPLE ARBITRATION AGREEMENT

Employer and Employee ("Employee") hereby agree as follows:

1. In accordance with the terms set forth below, Employer and Employee (collectively parties) shall participate in the Arbitration Process with respect to any and all Disputes or Claims they have, or may in the future have, against the other arising from or relating to their employment relationship.

2. Definitions

a. Disputes or Claims include, but are not limited to: (1) any dispute regarding the arbitrability of a dispute or claim; (2) Any dispute regarding this Agreement, including but not limited to its enforceability, scope or terms; (3) Any claim that could be asserted by an Employee against the Employer (or its employees, managers, directors, officers, affiliates, parents, successors, or assigns), or by Employer against the Employee, in any state or federal civil court or before an administrative agency, including without limitation, claims for breach of any contract or covenant, express or implied, invasion of privacy, breach of duty of loyalty, conversion, unjust enrichment, replevin, misappropriation, violation of any trade secret laws, defamation, infliction of emotional distress, tortious interference with contract, or other tort claims, including any claim that an employee was injured or damaged because of the negligence of the Employer or any of its employees; and claims for wrongful discharge and/or for violation of any federal, state or local statute, ordinance, regulation, or common law; (4) Any claim for discrimination under Title VII of the Civil Rights Act, the California Government Code, the Age Discrimination In Employment Act, the Americans with Disabilities Act, or any other law, including but not limited to claims for discrimination because of sex, pregnancy, race, national or ethnic origin, age, religion, creed, marital status, sexual harassment, sexual orientation, mental or physical disability or medical condition or other characteristics protected by law; (5) Any claim of retaliation or discrimination against the Employer for opposing the violation of any federal, state or local statute or ordinance or law; and (6) Any claim for commissions, wages, expenses, or penalties under the Fair Labor Standards Act, the California Labor Code, or any other federal, state, local, or common law. Disputes or Claims do not include claims for workers compensation benefits, claims for unemployment compensation benefits, or claims for benefits based upon the Employer's employee welfare benefit plans if the plan providing the employee benefit contains a final and binding appeal procedure for the resolution of disputes under the plan.

b. Arbitration. Means final and binding arbitration of the Dispute or Claim before an independent, impartial arbitrator selected either by the parties or in accordance with the procedures set forth by law.

3. In the event of a Dispute or Claim, the following Arbitration Process shall apply:

a. Any party to this Agreement may initiate arbitration by serving upon the other party, by certified mail, facsimile, or personal delivery a written notice containing a specific request to enter into arbitration. The written request shall identify and describe the nature of each claim asserted, the facts upon which each claim is based, and the relief or remedy sought. Written notice to the Employee will be sent to the most recent address contained in the Employee's personnel file. If, on the date that an arbitration demand is postmarked or received, any claim made in the demand would be barred by the applicable statute of limitations, that claim shall be deemed barred for purposes of arbitration.

b. Promptly after sending or receiving a written request to arbitrate, the Employer and Employee shall seek to agree upon an arbitrator. If the parties cannot reach agreement on an arbitrator, one will be selected in accordance with applicable law. The Employer shall bear all costs of the arbitrator and administrative costs associated with the arbitration, unless the arbitrator determines otherwise in accordance with applicable law.

c. Each party shall have the right to propound discovery and take depositions in accordance with the Federal Rules of Civil Procedure. The parties shall meet and confer in good faith in an attempt to resolve any discovery disputes. Any discovery disputes that cannot be resolved by the parties shall be resolved by the arbitrator.

d. The arbitrator shall have jurisdiction to hear and rule on pre-hearing disputes and motions (including dispositive motions) and is authorized to hold pre-hearing conferences by telephone or in person, as the arbitrator deems necessary. The arbitrator specifically shall have the authority to entertain motions to dismiss and/or motions for partial or complete summary judgment by any party and shall apply the standards governing such motions set by federal law.

e. Prior to the arbitration, in a time frame set by the arbitrator, the parties will exchange lists of witnesses, including any experts, and copies of all exhibits intended to be used at the arbitration. Each party shall have the right to subpoena witnesses and documents for the arbitration as well as documents relevant to the case from third parties.

f. If the Claim or Dispute is not otherwise resolved, the arbitrator shall preside at a hearing and rule on the admission and exclusion of evidence and questions of procedure, and exercise other such powers as conferred by law. The arbitrator shall have the authority and discretion to admit any relevant evidence if it is of the sort that reasonable persons are accustomed to rely on in the conduct of serious affairs, regardless of the admissibility of such evidence in a court of law.

g. The arbitrator shall apply the substantive law (and the law of remedies, if applicable) of the state in which the state law claim arose, or federal law of the circuit in which the federal law claim arose, or both, as applicable to the claim(s) asserted. The arbitrator is without jurisdiction to apply any different substantive law or law of remedies.

h. Each party shall bear his, her, or its own attorneys' fees and other costs not associated with the arbitrator or the administration of the arbitration. However, if a party is entitled to attorneys' fees under any federal, state or local statute or law, the arbitrator will award those fees pursuant to that law.

i. Should any party refuse or neglect to appear for, or participate in, the arbitration hearing, the arbitrator shall have the authority to decide the dispute based upon whatever evidence is presented.

j. Either party, at its expense, may arrange for and pay the cost of a court reporter to provide a stenographic record of proceedings.

k. Either party, upon request at the close of hearing, shall be given leave to file a post-hearing brief. The time for filing such a brief shall be set by the arbitrator at a reasonable time relative to the preparation of any transcript.

l. Within a reasonable time after submittal of the case, the arbitrator shall render a written award and opinion which is signed and dated and which decides all issues submitted as well as the legal principles supporting each part of the award . The arbitrator may grant any remedy or relief, legal or equitable, that would have been available had the claim been asserted in court. The award shall include a statement of the factual and legal bases for the ruling.

7. Either party may bring an action in any court of competent jurisdiction to compel arbitration under this Agreement and to enforce or set aside an arbitration award.

8. The parties understand that, through this Agreement, they waive their right to a jury or bench trial of their Disputes or Claims. However,

nothing in this Agreement is intended to preclude a party from seeking, or a court of competent jurisdiction from considering or granting, a provisional remedy of the type set forth in California Code of Civil Procedure §1281.2. Nothing in this Agreement is intended to prohibit Employee from filing a claim or communicating with any governmental agency, including the Equal Employment Opportunity Commission, the Department of Fair Employment and Housing, the Department of Labor, or the Department of Labor Standards and Enforcement.

9. Should any provision of this Agreement be found to be unenforceable, such portion will be severed from the Agreement and the remaining portions shall remain in full force and effect.

10. This is the complete agreement of the parties on the subject of arbitration of disputes. This Agreement supersedes any prior or contemporaneous oral or written understandings on the subject. No party is relying on any representations, oral or written on the subject of the effect, enforceability or meaning of this Agreement, except as specifically set forth in this Agreement.

11. The Employee's signature on the Agreement certifies that the Employee has carefully read this agreement and understands its terms. The Employee acknowledges that all understandings and agreements between the Employer and Employee relating to the subjects covered in the agreement are contained in it, and that the Employee has entered into the Agreement voluntarily and not in reliance on any promises or representations by the Employer other than those contained in this Agreement itself. The Employee further acknowledges that the Employee has been given the opportunity to discuss this Agreement with the Employee's private attorney.

EMPLOYEE:
By: ______________________________
Date: ____________________________
Printed Name: _______________________

Courtesy of Chris Baker, Thelen Reid Brown Raysman & Steiner LLP

APPENDIX C

SARBANES-OXLEY COMPLAINT PROCEDURES AND INVESTIGATION CHECKLIST

Employers may find it useful to consider the following reporting and investigation procedures with regard to a SOX whistleblower complaint:

- Adopt a written policy prohibiting discrimination and retaliation against SOX whistleblowers.

- Implement procedures for employees to report SOX complaints. These procedures could include:

    - Reporting a SOX complaint to an immediate supervisor or the human resources department.

    - Reporting a SOX complaint to the Company President or chief officer.

    - Reporting a SOX complaint to a member of the Company's audit committee.

    - Implementing an anonymous, toll-free SOX whistleblower hotline.

    - Distribute and educate employees regarding SOX complaint reporting procedures through the employee handbook, posters, training sessions, wallet cards, etc.

- Adopt a written policy that establishes specific steps the Company will take in response to a SOX complaint. The policy may include:

    - Procedures for forwarding any SOX complaint to the party responsible for investigation.

    - Procedures to ensure that all complaints of corporate misconduct are reported to the appropriate responsible parties.

- Procedures that will be taken by the persons responsible for investigating a SOX complaint.

- Advise and retain in-house and/or outside counsel to assist with the investigation.

- Procedures for determining who within the Company will be responsible for reviewing the results of the investigation and deciding whether further action is needed.

- Implement a procedure to apprise the complaining employee of any resolution.

- Implement training programs to educate managers, supervisors and employees regarding SOX complaints and the tools available to address employee concerns.

- Review SOX policies and procedures on a periodic basis to ensure compliance and maintain a commitment to take appropriate action with respect to any retaliation against a complaining employee, up to and including termination of employment.

Courtesy of Allegra Lawrence-Hardy, Sutherland Asbill & Brennan LLP

APPENDIX D

SAMPLE SARBANES-OXLEY ANTI-RETALIATION POLICY

ABC Company is firmly committed to conducting business with integrity and complying with any applicable provisions of the Sarbanes-Oxley Act of 2002 ("SOX"). To further the Company's commitment, any supervisor or managerial employee who receives a complaint regarding improper financial, accounting, auditing or reporting practices or alleged corporate misconduct *must* report it immediately. Employees may report the matter to the their immediate supervisor, the Human Resources department, or the Company President. While many employee complaints may not fall within the scope of SOX, it is the policy of ABC Company that all such complaints be reported so that the Company may determine whether further action is warranted. No employee will be disciplined or otherwise retaliated against for complaining of alleged corporate misconduct or improper financial, accounting, auditing or reporting practices.

All reports of corporate misconduct will be addressed by the Company in an appropriate manner. Confidentiality will be maintained during the investigation to the extent possible without jeopardizing the thoroughness of the investigation. Retaliation of any kind against the individual making the report is expressly prohibited. The Company will investigate the complaint and determine whether further action is warranted, and the employee making the complaint will be advised of the results of the investigation as may be appropriate under the circumstances of each complaint.

Courtesy of Allegra Lawrence-Hardy, Sutherland Asbill & Brennan LLP

ASPATORE